D1479426

THE
SQUARE-TO-SQUARE
GOLF
SWING
Modern Method for the Modern Player

THE
SQUAR

illustrated by **ANTHONY RAVIELLI**

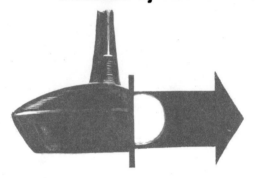

TO-SQUARE GOLF SWING

Model Method for the Modern Player

by DICK AULTMAN
and the Editors of GOLF DIGEST

COLLINS
St James's Place, London

William Collins Sons & Co Ltd
London · Glasgow · Sydney · Auckland
Toronto · Johannesburg

First published in United Kingdom 1971
Copyright © 1970 by Golf Digest, Inc.
ISBN 0 00 211798 3

Made and Printed in Great Britain by
William Collins Sons & Co Ltd Glasgow

FOREWORD

In the spring of 1968 I underwent the most profound experience of my golfing life. It occurred at a PGA Business School in Kansas City during an instruction seminar conducted by Jim Flick, head professional at the Losantiville Country Club in Cincinnati.

During his talk Flick contrasted the differences between the modern method of *pulling* the clubhead into the ball with the left hand, arm and side dominant, as opposed to the older technique of *throwing* the club on the downswing, largely with the right side. He explained how the so-called Square-to-Square swing—the more modern method—develops power by stretching the stronger muscles of the legs and back, rather than simply stressing the weaker muscles of the hands and arms. He showed how in the Square-to-Square swing the hands and clubhead move into the proper relationship for a powerful and square impact during the slower-moving takeaway, rather than during the faster-moving, less-controllable downswing.

Everything Flick said seemed very simple and logical to me. The Square-to-Square Method he described included points that other teachers who I respect, such as my brother, Jim, and Jack Burke, Jr., had stressed to me earlier. It seemed many of the motions Flick attributed to the relatively old-fashioned "throwing" swing were motions that I was making. Looking back on my golfing career, though I had won four PGA tournaments and quite a bit of money, I always had felt that my success resulted largely from my ability to putt well, rather than from a swing that produced consistently sound shots under pressure. As I listened to Flick, I became so convinced that the "pulling" swing was superior that I decided to take a year—maybe even two—to incorporate the Square-to-Square Method into my own game.

As I began the changeover in the weeks that followed, I realized that this modern swing could be, and should be, taught to the golfing masses. I had been looking for some meaningful way to "give back" some of the benefits that I had derived from golf; perhaps I could somehow make a contribution by converting other players and teaching professionals to the Square-to-Square swing.

I decided that I would not make a specific crusade of actually teaching the various aspects of the modern swing to others. This was being done already in excellent fashion by Flick, Bill Strausbaugh of the Columbia Country Club, Chevy Chase, Md., and other teaching professionals, largely through talks to fellow-professionals at PGA schools. Instead, I set out to learn just how this modern method had evolved. I hoped that the method itself would be more readily accepted by the game's teachers if I could discover, and explain logically, just why today's successful players are gradually discarding old techniques and replacing them with the Square-to-Square Method.

I started my research in the library of the United States Golf Ass'n in New York City. That first day at Golf House was probably as exciting a day as I've ever had in my life. As I read those old instruction books it became apparent that golfers of every era have been interested in the mechanics of the swing, probably since the very birth of the game in the 15th century. As I continued my reading and studying of old films during the off-seasons, it became evident to me that whenever a golfer moved ahead of his fellow-competitors —as had Vardon, Jones, Nelson, Hogan and Palmer—it was due largely to his discovering a superior swing method and using it to replace established techniques. Usually, the superior method was simpler; it had fewer moving parts—less chance to err. Usually the superior method made the best use of the type of equipment available at the time. Invariably the golfer who dominated with a superior method was copied by his peers and those who followed—until someone else moved away from the pack using a still-simpler, more-efficient technique.

Today, whenever it is at all possible, I present my findings to teaching professionals and players through lectures, blackboard diagrams and films of leading golfers from Vardon to present-day stars. I am convinced beyond doubt that the Square-to-Square swing is the simplest, most effective method yet devised to best use today's equipment. The path of evolution toward this method has been a logical process spawned by the constant drive for accuracy and distance, by the constant urge of all golfers to learn the secrets of their champions, and by the continual updating of equipment. I feel that the gradual transition from a "throwing" swing to a "pulling" swing is the last major change in this process, and that it has been brought about by the advent of steel shafts.

The classic "throwing" swing of Bobby Jones was most efficient because it allowed Jones to swing the flexible wooden shaft *quietly,* yet rapidly, and thereby minimize its bending and twisting. On the other hand, the less-flexible steel shaft allowed Nelson and Hogan to swing more *dynamically,* and thereby develop greater speed while still maintaining and increasing accuracy. In other words, the evolution continued as those golfers survived who had adapted most efficiently to the new "environment" of steel.

Obviously I am sold on the Square-to-Square Method as being the most up-to-date and efficient way to swing a golf club. I know that it is the method that works best for me. My victories during the past year in the Atlanta Classic, the Argentine Masters and the recent

Bing Crosby National Pro-Am, merely indicate to me that I'm doing a better job of applying Square-to-Square principles, and that these principles, being simpler, are more efficient under pressure.

I am delighted that GOLF DIGEST has made this book available to the golfing public. Not only does it explain a subject dear to my heart, but it presents Square-to-Square as a total concept. It relates each part of the Method to every other part and to the goals of the swing as a whole. The result is a book that brings new insight and meaning to the study of the golf swing. I think it represents a milestone in golf instruction and I recommend it wholeheartedly, not only to Mr. and Mrs. Average Golfer, but also to teaching professionals and my fellow-competitors on the tour.

Bert Yancey
March, 1970

CONTENTS

INTRODUCTION

The golfer, perhaps more than any other sportsman, continually searches for The Secret. He looks for that one adjustment in grip, stance or swing that will eliminate, immediately and forever, all sliced drives, topped fairway woods and "fat" approach shots, and that will—of course—add 15-20 yards to his tee shots.

Eventually, most serious golfers discover The Secret—at least a half-dozen times each summer. They rush to the course, or the driving range. Every shot flies straight and true and far. Watch out, Arnie! Move over, Jack! Here I come, Gary!

Then, after an hour or a day or a week, The Secret fails. The golfer dejectedly realizes that once again he's duped himself. He knows he must renew the struggle. He must find another panacea.

This book is not about another secret. Secrets usually don't last. Too often they lure, deceive, and then burst like bubbles. Nor is this a book of "corrective" teachings. It is not presented, for example, as a sure cure for slicing or hooking, though the reader may well reap such benefits. Instead, this book is about a *method*.

While secrets often fail and leave you stranded, and while "corrective" instruction cannot apply directly to a vast audience of golfers

WHEN YOUR HANDS ARE HIP-HIGH ON THE BACKSWING, IS YOUR LEFT WRIST...

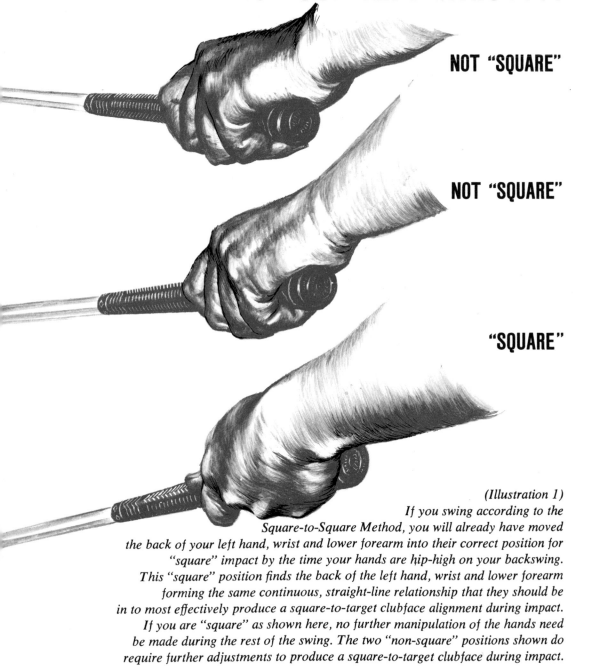

NOT "SQUARE"

NOT "SQUARE"

"SQUARE"

(Illustration 1)
If you swing according to the Square-to-Square Method, you will already have moved the back of your left hand, wrist and lower forearm into their correct position for "square" impact by the time your hands are hip-high on your backswing. This "square" position finds the back of the left hand, wrist and lower forearm forming the same continuous, straight-line relationship that they should be in to most effectively produce a square-to-target clubface alignment during impact. If you are "square" as shown here, no further manipulation of the hands need be made during the rest of the swing. The two "non-square" positions shown do require further adjustments to produce a square-to-target clubface during impact.

AT THE TOP OF YOUR BACKSWING, IS YOUR LEFT WRIST...

"SQUARE"

with varying swing faults, a method—once properly developed—can provide a widely varying group of players with a solid swing foundation that never will crumble. A good method incorporates sound fundamentals of gripping, setting up to the ball and swinging. It allows you to make long and relatively straight shots *consistently,* even under pressure.

This book is about the Square-to-Square Method, a way of playing golf that is gaining favor with increasing rapidity, not only among the game's top performers, but, more important, within the teaching profession that administers to the needs of millions of club players.

The principles involved in the Square-to-Square Method are not all new. So-called "square" techniques for hitting a golf ball began to evolve very slowly in the 1930s, gained momentum after World War II, and since have been at least partially adopted by most outstanding players, first on the U.S. Professional Golfers' Association (PGA) tour, then later by Far Eastern professionals who copied

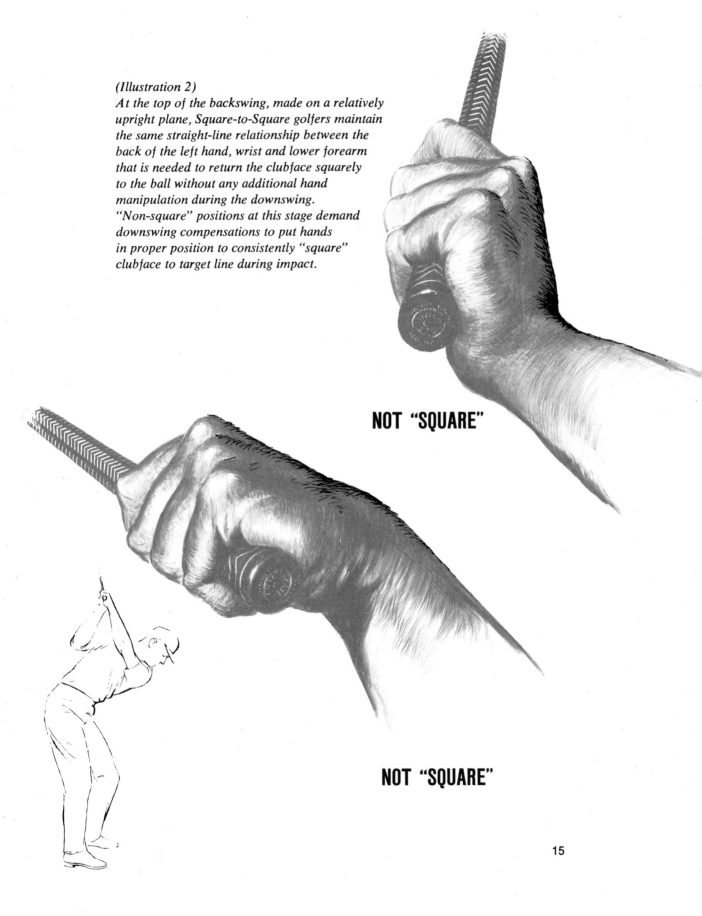

(Illustration 2)
At the top of the backswing, made on a relatively upright plane, Square-to-Square golfers maintain the same straight-line relationship between the back of the left hand, wrist and lower forearm that is needed to return the clubface squarely to the ball without any additional hand manipulation during the downswing.
"Non-square" positions at this stage demand downswing compensations to put hands in proper position to consistently "square" clubface to target line during impact.

NOT "SQUARE"

NOT "SQUARE"

15

American golf swing techniques just as astutely as many of their countrymen imitated U.S. manufacturing methods and general styles of living. More recently many of the top players of Great Britain have discarded traditional Scottish swing tendencies and now are beginning successfully to employ the Square-to-Square Method in part or in whole.

Such outstanding teachers and theoreticians of the golf swing as Percy Boomer, Jim and Joe Dante, J. Victor East, Paul Bertholy, Bill Ogden, Brodie Lennox, Dale Andreason, Irv Schloss, Bob Toski, Byron Nelson, Claude Harmon, and many others, have discussed various elements of the Square-to-Square Method in books and articles. As long as 15 years ago, in the July 1954 issue of GOLF DIGEST, amateur champion Dick Chapman and professional star Betty Hicks noted the increasing use of a Square-to-Square swing among leading players in their article, "Keep That Clubface Square." Mr. East's article, "Why the Americans Beat the British" (August, 1959) further boosted the Method, and stirred additional awakening among instructors around the world.

Today, in America particularly, the Square-to-Square Method, developed by the game's top players, is filtering down and influencing the swings of average club golfers. Increasingly, leaders of the golf teaching profession are studying and refining the Method and are teaching it to fellow-professionals through schools, seminars and clinics sponsored by the PGA. Leading college coaches such as Les Bolstad, Labron Harris, Sr., Henry Ransom, Conrad Rehling and many others are preaching Square-to-Square techniques to future stars.

Yet, though the Method has evolved to a high degree in the swings of many of the world's best golfers, though it has been discussed and partially promulgated in books and articles, and though it is being taught by professional instructors, it has never been presented in totality in the printed form.

The purpose of this book is to explain the Square-to-Square Method as a *total concept*. The editors of GOLF DIGEST feel that this explanation must necessarily involve detailed instruction about, for

DURING IMPACT,
IS YOUR LEFT WRIST...

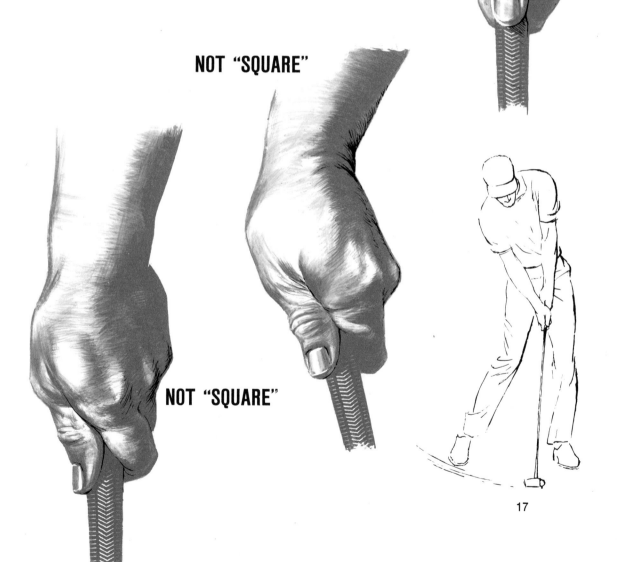

"SQUARE"

(Illustration 3)
In the Square-to-Square swing, the golfer returns the clubface
squarely to the ball with back of left hand, wrist and lower
forearm facing "square" to target line and still in
straight-line relationship needed for consistently solid blows.
"Non-square" positions invite misalignment of clubface
or collapse of left wrist when club encounters ball's resistance.

NOT "SQUARE"

NOT "SQUARE"

17

instance, correct gripping and setting up as well as actual swinging.

The editors of GOLF DIGEST feel that, *when taken as a total concept,* Square-to-Square is a way to play that offers excellent chances for success to any golfer who is serious about improving, and who is willing to work to achieve that goal. The Method is easy to understand because it is logical. For instance, it requires that the downswing tend to be—though not completely be—more of a pulling action by the left side than a pushing or throwing action of the right side. Though the throwing movement may be more *natural* —especially for those who have played "throwing" games as youths —the idea of pulling 10-15 pounds of hand and arm with 150 pounds of body is more *logical* than pushing 150 pounds of body with 10-15 pounds of hand and arm.

Let it be clearly understood, however, that though the Method can be learned by any golfer, it should be learned gradually, in stages, according to the ability of the pupil. The beginner or novice should regard this book largely as an explanation of the direction in which he will be moving, and the goals he will be seeking, *after* first learning to swing the clubhead rhythmically with good speed and reasonable control.

Learning the Method also requires dedication, even for the more-advanced golfer. Bear in mind that Square-to-Square is a method that is designed to last a lifetime. Learning it properly requires a transition period—often several weeks—during which time the normally-weaker, left-side muscles must be re-trained to dominate the normally-stronger, right-side muscles. During this period the golfer can expect bad shots and loss of distance as he or she discards the comfort and familiarity of right-side control. Skills will gradually return, and eventually surpass previous levels, but only after the superiority of left-side control comes to the fore.

Many members of the golf teaching profession, too numerous to mention, were helpful in the preparation of this book. Special recognition, however, must be given to Jim Flick, head professional, Losantiville Country Club, Cincinnati, O., and president of the

Southern Ohio PGA Section, and to Bill Strausbaugh, Jr., head professional at Columbia Country Club, Chevy Chase, Md., and PGA Golf Professional of the Year for 1966, for the countless hours that they spent cooperating with the editors.

It was Flick, a leading spokesman for the Square-to-Square Method in teaching programs of the Professional Golfers' Ass'n and the National Golf Foundation, who first brought the idea of doing a magazine article on the Method to the attention of GOLF DIGEST President Bill Davis in the winter of 1967-68. Flick stayed at the Golf Digest House at Augusta, Ga., during the 1968 Masters, working with this writer on the proposed article. Flick's enthusiasm for the subject and obvious knowledge of the golf swing impressed all of the editors, and before long the article had mushroomed, first into a series, and then, finally, this book.

During the actual writing process, both Flick and Strausbaugh studied the various chapters and made constructive suggestions. Pete Zangrillo, owner of the Darien (Conn.) Golf Range, an outstanding instructor and a staunch supporter of Square-to-Square principles, gave us all a large measure of enthusiastic support during this period.

Other GOLF DIGEST people who helped prepare this book were Bill Davis, Publisher Howard Gill, Jr., General Manager Jack Barnett, Editorial Director Ken Bowden and Managing Editor Larry Sheehan, all of whom read and improved the text with words and illustrative ideas, and Editorial Assistant Barbara Kelly who never complained about re-typing manuscripts seemingly countless times.

The precise detail of the book's illustrations reflects the burgeoning interest in Square-to-Square of Anthony Ravielli, who is regarded as the world's leading golf artist, having illustrated Ben Hogan's *Modern Fundamentals of Golf* and the recent *Bobby Jones on the Basic Golf Swing*. As does this writer, Tony eagerly awaits the passing of this New England winter so that he can personally apply the principles he has illustrated.

Dick Aultman, Editor, GOLF DIGEST
Norwalk, Conn., January, 1970

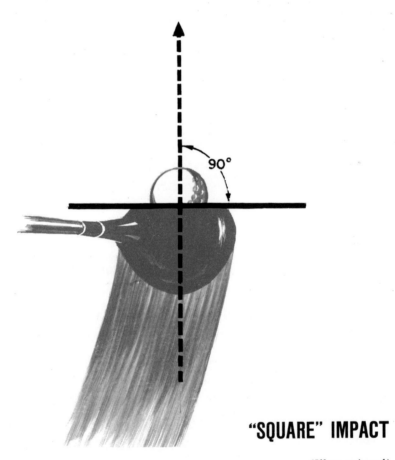

"SQUARE" IMPACT

(Illustration 4)
*If clubface looks directly down the target line during impact, it is considered
"square," because the clubface itself forms a 90-degree, or "square," angle with
the target line. To make a "perfect" golf shot, the clubface must be "square"
during impact. It also must be moving along the target line at maximum speed.*

CHAPTER
ONE

SQUARE-TO-SQUARE
WHAT IT IS, WHAT IT CAN DO

To make a "perfect" golf shot certain mechanical requirements must be met during impact—that split second when the ball is being squashed against the clubface.

First, the clubface must be "looking" down the line along which the golfer intends that the ball should fly. When the clubface does look down the target line during impact, it is considered "square." It forms a 90-degree, or "square," angle to that line (*see illustration 4*). If, during impact, the clubface is looking either to the right or the left of the intended line of flight, the ball can *never* fly along the path that the golfer has chosen (although it may reach the target via a hooking or slicing route).

Second, in order to execute a "perfect" golf shot the clubhead must be moving *along* the intended line—and at ball level in the case of the tee shot—as it strikes the ball. If it is not moving along this line, if it is traveling from outside or inside this line during impact, the clubhead, depending on how it is facing, will either push the shot to the right or pull it to the left, or strike the ball a glancing blow and apply some degree of sidespin. The glancing blow not only reduces force—and thus the distance of the shot—but it also causes the ball to spin off to left or right of the target line.

Third, the "perfect" golf shot, to travel its fullest distance, must be struck with the maximum amount of clubhead speed that the golfer can generate.

How often does a golfer meet these three requirements—square clubface, on-line clubhead path and maximum clubhead speed? Some players almost never achieve such perfection. The very best obtain it infrequently. Ben Hogan has been quoted as saying that during a good round he probably hits no more than one or two full shots that really felt 100 per cent.

However, there are degrees of success in golf. The golfer who shoots in the middle 80s probably takes about 40 "full" shots with iron or wood clubs during his average round. The rest of his strokes are made on and around the greens. Of his 40 full shots, he may hit 4 or 5 that feel relatively solid, that set up a sure par or a possible birdie. He'll dub a half-dozen or more and take a bogey, or worse. The rest of his shots will not feel quite right, but they won't cause him too much trouble.

Those professionals who teach the Square-to-Square Method feel that it is the ideal technique to increase your chances of impacting full shots with a clubhead that is: (1) facing "square" to the intended line, (2) moving along that line and, (3) traveling at maximum speed. They stress that the degree to which you master the Method will determine directly the degree of perfection and consistency you will achieve in your shotmaking.

There are several ways in which the Square-to-Square Method promotes "square" clubface, on-line clubhead path and maximum clubhead speed during impact. These advantages of the Method will be explained shortly. The explanation will be more meaningful, however, if we first look briefly at just what Square-to-Square means and how it evolved as the most-favored method of the top modern players.

HOW THE SQUARE-TO-SQUARE SWING EVOLVED

The early golfers, those who set the swing patterns for future generations, played the game with wooden-shafted clubs. These shafts were very flexible, or "soft," by modern standards and had a tendency to allow the clubface to twist open during the swing. This twisting, or torque, action made it difficult to square the clubface with the target line during impact. Only by relying on their hands and wrists to roll the clubface back to a square position could the golfing pioneers hit straight shots with much consistency.

Thus, our ancestors became largely "hands" players. During their backswings many right-handed golfers would rotate the clubhead with a clockwise turning of the hands and forearms *(illustration 5)*. The left hand would more-or-less roll over the right, and the toe of the clubhead would turn away from the ball in advance of the heel. On the downswing these golfers could square up the clubface and thus hit straight-flying shots only if they reversed the procedure by rolling their hands and forearms in a counterclockwise manner. They found that by gripping the club with the right hand turned well to the right, more under the clubshaft, it was easier to maneuver the clubface back to a square position at impact. To this day there are golf instructors who still believe, scientific data to the contrary, that a player can add considerable distance to shots by consciously turning the clubhead in a counterclockwise manner as it moves through the hitting area.

The early golfers not only controlled the clubface position largely by hand manipulation, but they also found it simpler anatomically— more "natural"—to swing the club on a relatively horizontal, or "flat," plane. Their shoulders tended to turn on a plane that was more akin to a merry-go-round than to a Ferris wheel. A major reason for this flat swing was that it helped them give the ball the low, hooking, fast-running trajectory favored for the windy ocean-side links of England and Scotland.

During the 1930s and after World War II, however, certain developments occurred in golf, largely in America, that caused

(Illustration 5)

Largely because of the twisting characteristics of wooden-shafted clubs, early golfers were forced to manipulate the club with their hands in order to square the clubface with the target line during impact. These players gripped the club with their hands turned far to the right on the shaft in a so-called "strong" position to better allow them to "roll" their clubface into a square position with a counterclockwise turning of the hands as they moved into the hitting area. This procedure prohibits the clubface from looking down and moving along the target line for as long a duration as is possible with modern metal-shafted clubs.

players to seek a simpler, more reliable method of striking a golf ball.

Because of automatic sprinkling systems, American courses became wetter and lusher, which led to an increase in ball diameter (to the present 1.68 inches). The tendency of this larger ball to rise more easily than the 1.62-inch ball that most other countries continued to favor, diminished the need for hand action—the Scottish "flick-the-clubhead" technique—during the downswing. American players discovered that they achieved greater control over the height and accuracy of shots with a body-oriented swing that "pulled" the clubhead solidly and smoothly through the hitting area.

The advent concurrently of steel shafts, which had less tendency to twist and bend, also greatly lessened the need for manipulation of the clubhead with the hands. Led by the American professionals, golfers found that the less they rotated the club clockwise with their hands and forearms during the backswing, the less they needed to compensate with counterclockwise movement on the downswing to square the clubface at impact. By minimizing the moving parts (hands and forearms) they found that they minimized the chances for error.

And then, perhaps catalyzing all the other factors, was the matter of distance, the urge and the necessity to hit a golf ball ever farther. The larger ball needed more forceful, accurate striking if it were to travel as far as its predecessors. Courses were getting longer and more "holding." Incentives grew greater and competition tougher on the professional tour. Success began to depend more and more on sheer yardage and less and less on finesse. And the steel shafts would take all the stresses that the most Herculean players could apply.

Golfers like Byron Nelson, the most-notable example, pioneered aspects of the new method. Unlike most of their peers who still "threw" the clubhead with their hands—a technique that had proven highly successful with wooden-shafted clubs—they took the accent off hands and put it on the bigger muscles of the body, especially those of the back and legs, the major sources of athletic power. Arnold Palmer, Jack Nicklaus and many others—even more power-conscious—carried the new techniques into the '60s, improving on them as they went.

WHAT IS "SQUARE-TO-SQUARE"?

For years the position of the golfer's clubface at the top of his or her backswing has been described as being "closed," "open" or "square."

If the clubface looks more or less straight up to the sky it is considered "closed" *(illustration 6)*. Many golfers, and some teachers, feel that from such a position the golfer must make some sort of compensation during the downswing in order for the clubface to be "square"—looking down the target line—during impact. Theoretically, if such compensation is not made, the clubface will remain in a closed position so that it looks to the left of target when it contacts the ball. The golfer who swings from a "closed" clubface position at the top of his swing to a "square" clubface position at impact is said to have a "closed-to-square" swing.

The so-called "open" position at the top of the backswing finds the clubface looking more or less straight out, in the same direction the golfer is facing. Many golfers and teachers believe that from this position the golfer must make a different sort of compensatory movement on the downswing to avoid an "open" face at impact. Such a swing would be designated "open-to-square."

If at the top of the swing the clubface is positioned about midway between "closed" and "open," it is considered "square." From a square clubface position at the top of the swing, the golfer can, theoretically, return to a square impact position without any compensatory movements. Many golfers consider this to be a "square-to-square" swing.

However, those who teach the Square-to-Square Method do not follow the old system of assigning designations of "closed," "square" and "open" to *clubface* positions. These teachers feel that judging the swing on the basis of clubface positions has been misleading to both pupils and instructors.

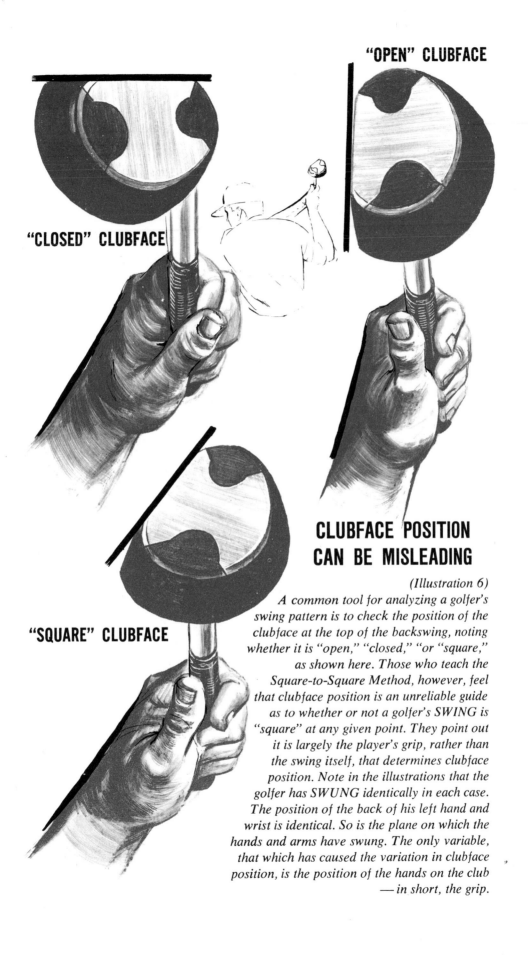

"OPEN" CLUBFACE

"CLOSED" CLUBFACE

"SQUARE" CLUBFACE

CLUBFACE POSITION CAN BE MISLEADING

(Illustration 6)

A common tool for analyzing a golfer's swing pattern is to check the position of the clubface at the top of the backswing, noting whether it is "open," "closed," "or "square," as shown here. Those who teach the Square-to-Square Method, however, feel that clubface position is an unreliable guide as to whether or not a golfer's SWING is "square" at any given point. They point out it is largely the player's grip, rather than the swing itself, that determines clubface position. Note in the illustrations that the golfer has SWUNG identically in each case. The position of the back of his left hand and wrist is identical. So is the plane on which the hands and arms have swung. The only variable, that which has caused the variation in clubface position, is the position of the hands on the club — in short, the grip.

For instance, three golfers with identical address positions and backswings can achieve three entirely different clubface positions at the top of their swings if they each grip the club in a different manner. The golfer who grips with his hands turned far to the right on the clubshaft—the so-called "strong" grip position—will normally present a very "closed" clubface position at the top of his swing. The golfer who makes the *same* backswing, but who grips with a very "weak" grip—hands positioned far to the left—will present a very "open" clubface position at the top of his swing. Because one's grip so greatly influences clubface positioning, it is not reliable to use such positioning to indicate if a player's swing is "square."

Also, the *plane* of a golfer's swing can alter the position of the clubface at the top. Three golfers with identical grips and identical backswings can arrive at three entirely different clubface positions because of the variance in the plane of their backswings. The golfer who has a very "flat" backswing, who swings more like a merry-go-round than a Ferris wheel, tends to arrive at a relatively closed clubface position at the top of the backswing. The golfer with an upright swing—more like a Ferris wheel than a merry-go-round—tends to produce an open clubface position at the top.

You can prove this to yourself. While looking in a mirror, merely swing back on an intentionally flat plane and note the position of the clubface at the top of your swing. From that position move your hands to a point high over your shoulders, where they would be if you had swung on a very upright plane *(illustration 7)*. Note how the clubface becomes more "open" as you change the position of your hands and arms.

Thus, clubface position at the top of the backswing is not a reliable measure of the effectiveness of the player's backswing. Nor does a square clubface at the top of the backswing necessarily assure a square face during impact.

Because a golfer's grip and swing plane can distort the true meaning of clubface position (other factors such as length of backswing also affect clubface positioning), progressive instructors prefer to

relatively
"CLOSED"

relatively
"OPEN"

another reason why
CLUBFACE POSITION CAN BE
MISLEADING

(Illustration 7)
*In illustration 6 it was shown that the nature of a
golfer's grip can largely determine the position
of the clubface during his swing. Therefore, it was
noted, clubface position at the top of the backswing,
whether it be "open," "closed," or "square," is not a reliable guide to how the
player actually swings the club. Another reason why clubface position is an
unreliable guide is shown here. Note that the position of the clubface changes from
"relatively closed" to "relatively open" merely by swinging on a more upright plane
—more like a Ferris wheel than a merry-go-round. Those who teach the
Square-to-Square Method prefer to use other indicators than clubface position
in judging whether or not a player is "square" at any given point in the swing.*

29

describe the proper "square" position in a different manner. Generally, they refer to the "square" position as pertaining to *the relationship between the back of the left hand, wrist and lower forearm while swinging in proper plane.* When the back of the left hand, wrist and lower forearm form a *straight line,* the golfer is considered to be in a "square" position, if he is swinging on a sufficiently upright plane. This position is called "square" because it is the ideal position that the left hand, wrist and forearm should be in during a "square" impact *(illustration 8).*

In the true Square-to-Square swing now being used by the leading players and taught by progressive professionals, this straight-line relationship of the back of the left hand, wrist and forearm is established either when gripping the club, or during the early stages of the backswing. Thereafter it is firmly maintained through impact with absolutely no independent hand manipulation at any point during the swing.

Thus, in the true Square-to-Square swing, the golfer actually establishes his proper "square impact" position of left hand, wrist and lower forearm at the start of his swing, and then he merely retains this "square" position as he brings his bigger leg and back muscles into the shot. Hence, the designation "Square-to-Square."

It is important to understand that in the Square-to-Square swing the hands, wrists

THE "SQUARE" POSITION

(Illustration 8)
*Along with a proper grip, one vital facet of the
Square-to-Square Method is that the back
of the left hand, wrist and lower forearm must
form a straight-line relationship from early in
the backswing until well after impact. This
straight-line relationship (shown here at impact)
is known as the "square position" because,
if maintained through impact, it assures that
the clubface will be "square" to the target line
when the ball is struck. Because the golfer
should move into this square position early in
the backswing and maintain it through impact,
the Method itself is labelled "Square-to-Square."*

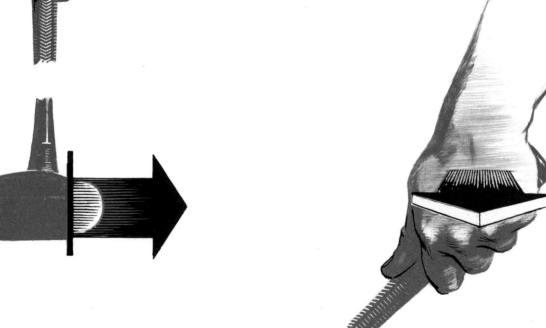

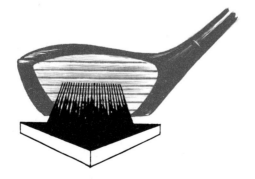

and arms are like the connecting rods linking the engine to the rear axle in a car. They do not *create* much power, but merely transmit it. The stronger muscles of the back and legs are the prime power sources—the "engine" of the swing.

Thus we have seen that the Square-to-Square Method involves *establishing and maintaining a constant straight-line relationship between the back of the left hand, wrist and lower forearm.* The Method also requires, however, that this straight-line, "square impact" position be established and maintained *while the golfer is turning his shoulders on a proper plane.*

"PROPER PLANE"

When one hears someone say of a golfer's swing that it is too "flat" or too "upright," that person is referring to the player's "swing plane." An extreme example of a "flat," or horizontal, plane is that of a baseball player swinging at a shoulder-high pitch. A merry-go-round also turns on a flat plane. To take the other extreme, a Ferris wheel turns on a perfectly "upright," or vertical, plane.

The plane of a golf swing falls somewhere between perfectly "flat" and perfectly "upright." The exact plane on which a golfer swings is dictated largely by the distance he stands from the ball. The farther away the ball is from the golfer's feet, the flatter—more horizontal—will be his swing plane. When driving, the golfer stands relatively far from the ball because he is using the longest club in the bag. On short-iron shots he stands closer to the ball simply because he is using a shorter club. Thus the plane of a swing with a driver is flatter than that with, say, a 9-iron. Unusually tall golfers tend to address shots with the ball closer to their feet than do relatively short golfers. Thus tall golfers naturally swing on a more upright plane than do short players.

The amount that a golfer bends forward at the waist also influences his or her swing plane. The more you bend forward—so long as your back remains relatively straight—the more upright will be your swing plane. To take two extremes, if a golfer did not bend at all from the waist—stood perfectly upright—to turn his body at all he would have to turn his shoulders and move the club on a more-or-less perfectly horizontal plane. A golfer who bent so much at the waist that his back was parallel to the ground would tend to swing on practically a perfectly upright or vertical plane.

For the plane of a golfer's swing to be "proper" in terms of the Square-to-Square Method, it must accomplish two things. First, it must enable the player to maintain *with relative ease* the straight line "square" relationship of the back of the left hand, wrist and the lower forearm that is a key part of the Square-to-Square Method. Generally, a more upright swing plane allows golfers to maintain such a relationship with less physical effort than does a flat swing plane.

The second requirement of a proper swing plane is that it allows the golfer to move the clubhead *along the target line and at ball level* for the longest possible duration at the bottom of the downswing. Obviously, the longer the club is moving toward the target and at ball level in the hitting area of the swing—the longer it stays on the so-called "flight path"—the greater will be the golfer's chances of striking the ball squarely.

It would be simple to keep the clubhead moving along the target line if one could swing on a perfectly upright, or vertical, plane like that of the Ferris wheel. In fact, a clubhead that moved on such a plane would *always* be over the target line *(illustration 9)*. Obviously, such a swing plane is physically impossible for a golfer to execute. Also, even if a golfer could swing perfectly upright, he would find that, as his clubhead moved through the hitting area, it was at *ball level* for too short a duration to make solid contact consistently.

On the other extreme, a perfectly flat, or horizontal, swing plane is also physically impossible for the golfer to produce, unless he could lay down on the grass and swing so that his clubhead never left the ground. If he could swing on such a plane—like that of a merry-go-round—he would indeed keep his club at ball level through-out his swing, but the clubhead would be moving along the target

EXTREME SWING PLANES

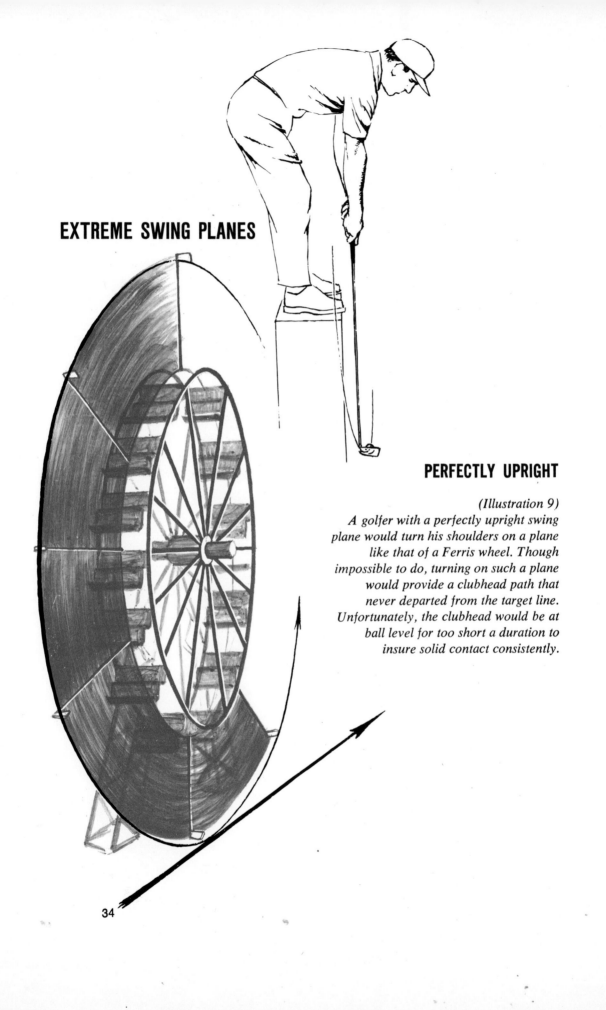

PERFECTLY UPRIGHT

(Illustration 9)
A golfer with a perfectly upright swing plane would turn his shoulders on a plane like that of a Ferris wheel. Though impossible to do, turning on such a plane would provide a clubhead path that never departed from the target line. Unfortunately, the clubhead would be at ball level for too short a duration to insure solid contact consistently.

line for only a fractional part of its travel—too short a duration for the golfer to achieve solid, square impact *(illustration 10)*.

The "proper" swing plane as defined under the Square-to-Square Method tends to be more vertical than horizontal. Not only does the more upright plane allow the player to retain the straight-line "square" position with relative ease—especially at the top of the swing—but it also keeps the clubhead moving along the target line for a relatively longer duration than would a flatter swing plane. The more upright swing does demand strong left-side control, however. Most players should move gradually toward such a plane only as their left-side control increases, say those who teach the Square-to-

PERFECTLY FLAT

(Illustration 10)
A golfer with a perfectly flat swing plane would turn his shoulders like a merry-go-round spins. Though such a swing plane is unrealistic, it would keep the clubhead moving at ball level throughout the swing. However, clubhead would not be moving along target line long enough to insure solid contact consistently.

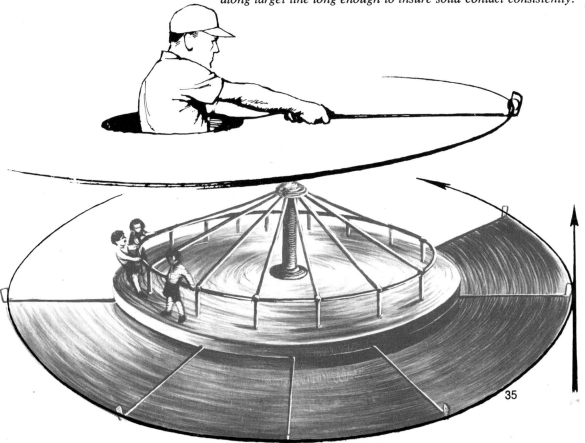

35

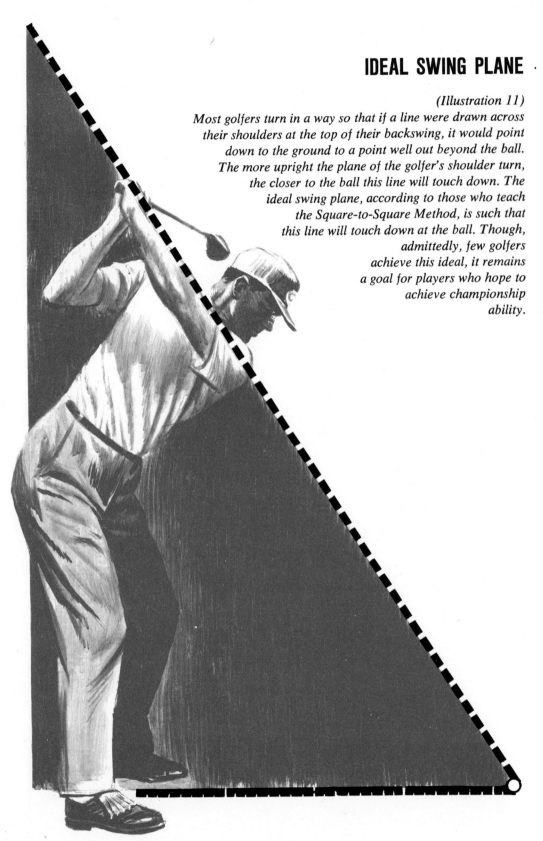

IDEAL SWING PLANE

(Illustration 11)

Most golfers turn in a way so that if a line were drawn across their shoulders at the top of their backswing, it would point down to the ground to a point well out beyond the ball. The more upright the plane of the golfer's shoulder turn, the closer to the ball this line will touch down. The ideal swing plane, according to those who teach the Square-to-Square Method, is such that this line will touch down at the ball. Though, admittedly, few golfers achieve this ideal, it remains a goal for players who hope to achieve championship ability.

Square Method. They reason that a shot made with a club that is not quite at ball level will merely fly higher or lower than normal. However, if the clubhead is not moving along the target line during impact, it will cause the shot to fly left or right of the intended line. Later chapters will elaborate on swing plane and explain how to make yours conform more closely to the ideal plane.

Now, having defined the Square-to-Square swing as being *the establishment and maintenance of a straight-line relationship between the back of the left hand and wrist and lower forearm while swinging on a proper plane,* let us enumerate some of the advantages of such a swing.

Readers are cautioned, however, not to try changing their swing planes without first mastering Square-to-Square Method principles involving posture and backswing. As indicated by the illustrations, the swing plane with a wood club normally is flatter than that with a short iron because the ball is played farther away from the feet with the longer-shafted club.

ADVANTAGES OF THE SQUARE-TO-SQUARE SWING

The Square-to-Square swing evolved because leading players sought an "edge" over their fellow-competitors. Players who learn this Method today will enjoy the same edge over those who employ less effective methods. The advantages derived from employing the Square-to-Square Method include:

1. A better chance for square contact with the ball, because the clubface "looks" down the target line for a greater duration of time and space as it moves through the hitting area.

2. More distance as a result of "squarer" contact of the clubface on the ball.

3. More distance through greater use of the large muscles of the back and legs, rather than the smaller muscles of the hands, wrists and arms.

4. More distance through greater retention of clubhead speed through impact, because the Method stresses and generates a stronger left side. The right side has less chance to take over and dissipate clubhead speed before impact.

5. More consistency because of less manipulation of the club with the hands and wrists. The swing is simpler because it uses fewer moving parts. This means that the golfer's timing and rhythm need not be absolutely perfect in order to produce relatively solid hits.

6. Greater control because the golfer works the club and the hands toward proper impact position during the slower-moving backswing, rather than during the faster-moving downswing.

7. Elimination of slicing caused by failure to rotate the clubhead back to a square position during downswing.

8. Elimination of hooking caused by collapse of the left wrist during impact.

And, finally, learning the Square-to-Square Method provides the golfer with a definite, clearcut avenue towards improvement. It enables him to know, always, *exactly what he is trying to do*. This, as all golfers whose games are now based on constant experimentation will appreciate, is a major psychological plus-factor, and a great stimulus to working for improvement.

Some professionals think of their pupils as being either Stage I, Stage II, or Stage III players. Generally a male Stage I player cannot break 100 for 18 holes on a course of over 6,000 yards. Stage II players will normally shoot in the 90s and middle-to-high 80s. Stage III players shoot in the low 80s and better. Though the scoring ranges would be higher, women can be similarly categorized.

The Square-to-Square Method is least applicable to the Stage I golfer. Such a player—especially if he is a beginner—usually faces the basic problem of putting the club in motion—of making a fluid, fast swing of the clubhead. Such players need first to develop freedom of movement, the sense of swinging the club. To this end, the Stage I golfer might benefit from more freedom of leg and lower-body movement during the backswing than is advocated in Chapters 3 and 4. He should allow himself to swing on a flatter swing plane— if that seems natural to him—than is advocated for the true Square-to-Square golfer. Before moving to a more upright plane, the Stage I golfer must develop a certain amount of left-side control. This will not occur for most until they have reached Stage II. Certainly, no Stage I golfer should attempt to execute the "curling under" movement described in Chapter 4 unless he is being supervised by a competent professional.

In short, for the Stage I golfer this book is designed merely to instill certain tendencies and thought patterns—such as the tendency to use the legs as well as merely the hands and arms—so that he may more readily apply specific Square-to-Square techniques at a later stage of development. The Stage II golfer can *gradually* move towards the Square-to-Square ideals advocated in this book. The Stage III player may apply the Method as it is presented in the text, so long as he or she also pays attention to the various "pitfalls" mentioned.

The editors of GOLF DIGEST would like to make it clear to those readers who choose to follow and apply the Method that any major overhaul of one's golf swing necessarily involves both a fair amount of practice as well as some—hopefully occasional—periods of discouragement. Learning the Square-to-Square Method calls for re-training muscles so that the normally weaker left hand, arm and side can dominate the normally stronger right hand, arm and side. However, those who teach Square-to-Square stress that rewards are commensurate with the efforts of the pupil to learn and develop the technique. The golfer who gives only minimal effort will, indeed, receive some benefit for his or her efforts. Partial learning is better than none, in this case. For pupils who are willing to go all the way, there is no limit to the amount they can improve.

The chapters that follow are presented in a manner the editors feel will minimize misunderstanding. Initially, each chapter will explain major goals and tell how accomplishing these goals relates to the swing as a whole. For instance, the discussion about posture will first explain how it affects such things as the plane of the swing, the golfer's ability to maintain the square position at the top of his swing, and how proper posture enables the player to fully stretch the big, power-producing muscles of the back and legs.

After explaining the goals and relating them to the total Square-to-Square concept, each chapter will then detail methods to achieve these goals. This "how to" portion will necessarily include elaboration on certain pitfalls that some golfers may encounter at this stage of his or her learning.

Next, each chapter will tell how the positions and movements described therein should look and *feel* to the reader if he or she has executed the instructions properly.

Finally, each chapter will conclude with a brief summary that will point up those key points that the golfer should have clear in his mind before proceeding on to the next phase of the Method.

The professionals who teach the Square-to-Square swing also have found that it is best if pupils start with short shots, then gradually move toward full-shot swings with the longer-shafted clubs.

By starting with chip shots, you will be able to concentrate on the fundamentals of grip and set-up and backswing without concern about adding distance. Also, you will be able physically to handle the shorter clubs more easily during the early stages when you are "teaching" left-side muscles to control your swing.

After learning to apply Square-to-Square methods to short chip shots, and after any changes in grip and address position begin to feel normal, you can then beneficially proceed to full shots with a 9-iron. Move on to full shots with longer irons only after you can swing the 9-iron through impact and beyond with the square position of the left hand and forearm remaining intact.

Finally, those who teach the Square-to-Square swing would warn that learning the Method will necessarily cause most players to alter old familiar habits. Because alterations in grip, address posture and the swing require conscious mental direction, your swing may lose much of its smoothness. Don't be discouraged when it happens.

Some players will hit shots to the right of target for a time after they first apply Square-to-Square techniques. This is a sign that the right side is still dominant. The right hand is either fanning open the clubface during the backswing or taking over control at the top of the swing. Hitting to the right will disappear as the left hand, arm and side learn to control the club.

Some golfers will run into the problem of hitting behind the ball on occasion. This too is caused by a loss of left-hand and left-side control at the top of the backswing, which forces the right hand-arm-shoulder quadrant to initiate the downswing.

Changes in grip, address position and swing also cause unfamiliar sensations that will make you feel insecure. At times as you address the ball, it may seem impossible that you can make a successful shot. You will be tempted to allow the image of a bad shot to creep into your mind's eye. Square-to-Square instructors advise that you consciously replace these negative images by visualizing the flight pattern of a successful shot. Visualizing successful shots is a technique by which leading golfers allow their subconscious to direct their muscles and nerves toward making a successful swing. Such visualization is even more important to the learning golfer.

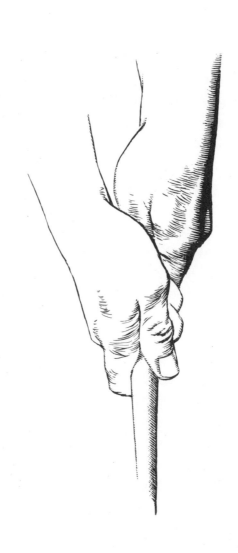

CHAPTER
TWO

THE GRIP MUST
CONTRIBUTE TO THE SWING

If you watch a baby eating, you may notice that the infant grasps its spoon or fork largely in the palm of its hand. Later in life the child will learn that it can do a much more efficient job of manipulating food from plate to mouth by holding the eating utensil in its fingers, instead of grasping it with the palm.

However, should the same child later develop into a husky shot-put champion, he will soon discover that it is much easier to rest a 16-pound shot in the palm of the hand, than to hold it in the fingers.

The point to be made here is that whenever a person uses his or her hands to hold, manipulate or throw an object, there is always a *preferred* way to grip the object in question. The way that we hold the object depends not only on its weight and size, but also on what we intend to do with it—the *goal* we seek to achieve.

If our goal in swinging a golf club were merely to hold onto it, we'd probably grip as tightly as possible, largely with our palms, as if we were swinging a sledgehammer. But merely holding on is not the only goal in swinging a golf club. There are other goals, and the way a golfer grips the club will determine, to a large degree, whether or not he or she will realize these goals.

5 GOALS OF PROPER GRIPPING

First let us look at some of the goals of the Square-to-Square swing that are directly affected by how you hold the club. If we bear in mind these goals, then we will be able to better understand why advocates of the Square-to-Square Method prescribe the grip that they do.

One major goal of the Square-to-Square swing is to consistently return the clubhead to the ball so that the clubface is *looking down the target line* during impact. If the clubface is looking to the right or left of this target line during impact, it will either (1) strike the ball a glancing blow and impart sidespin; or (2) strike the ball more or less solidly but push it to the right or pull it to the left. In any case, there is no way that a golfer can consistently hit shots along his intended line unless the clubface looks down that line during impact. One way to help make sure that the clubface consistently looks down the target line during impact is to grip in a manner that allows the back of the left hand, wrist and lower forearm to also face *down that line during impact*. The back of the left hand, wrist and lower forearm, like the clubface, should be "square" to the target line during impact.

Thus, we have our first guideline for proper gripping—to hold the club in a manner that best allows the back of the left hand, wrist and lower forearm—and the clubface—to be "square" to the target line during impact.

A second goal of the Square-to-Square swing is to "pull" the clubhead through the ball as fast as possible while still retaining complete control over its face alignment and plane. Because of certain anatomical considerations, a grip that allows the back of the left hand to be facing down the target line, rather than towards the sky, during impact is less likely to inhibit the transfer of force to the clubhead.

A third goal of the Square-to-Square swing is to turn the shoulders (and thus swing the club) on a relatively upright plane —more like a Ferris wheel than a merry-go-round. As pointed out in our earlier discussion of swing plane, the more upright the plane, the longer the clubhead moves *along* the target line through the hitting area, and the longer it moves on line, the greater the chances for straight shots. Therefore the proper grip, according to the Square-to-Square Method, is one that encourages swinging the club on a relatively upright swing plane.

A fourth goal inherent in the Square-to-Square swing is to avoid any fanning open of the clubface during the backswing through independent manipulation by the hands. We do not want the toe of the club moving away from the ball in advance of the heel. Such opening of the clubface was a feature of the early golfers' swings, a feature that forced compensatory manipulation of the club on the downswing in order to achieve a "square" clubface position during impact. Therefore, a fourth guideline is to grip in a manner that minimizes any tendency to fan the clubface during the backswing.

Finally, we will need to hold onto the club throughout the swing. There must not be any slipping of the club in the hands. We need a grip that will give us this control.

Thus we have established five criteria for a proper grip. It must allow the back of our left hand—and thus the clubface—to face "square" to the target line during impact. It must enable us to swing the clubhead fast through the ball. It must encourage us to swing on a relatively upright plane. It must disallow our fanning open the clubface. Finally, it must allow us to firmly hold onto, and thus control, the club throughout the swing.

PITFALL. *Before describing the correct grip for the Square-to-Square swing, we must caution that* any *change of grip may produce a feeling of discomfort or uneasiness, especially for veteran players who have become deeply accustomed to a certain grip. Most golfers will find that even a slight grip modification feels strange at first. With practice over a period of time, however, the new grip will soon feel as normal, and as comfortable, as did the old way of holding the club.*

HOW TO POSITION YOUR HANDS

Considering that the first grip goal you seek to reach is to square the back of the left hand to the target line during impact, it would seem logical to hold the club with the left hand in this position as you address the ball. Such a grip would find the left thumb on top of the shaft. As they addressed the ball, most golfers would see no left-hand knuckles other than those of the thumb and forefinger *(illustration 12)*.

Actually, this *is* the "ideal" grip position for the left hand at address. It is the position used by so many of today's professionals and long-advocated by Square-to-Square practitioners such as Tommy Bolt. Such positioning puts the clubface, left hand and lower-left forearm into proper "impact" relationship as advocated by those who teach the Square-to-Square Method. This is the relationship that, ideally, remains constant during the swing.

However, very few golfers should switch immediately to this positioning of the left hand in their grip. Only those golfers who are already at, or near, such positioning should attempt to grip in such

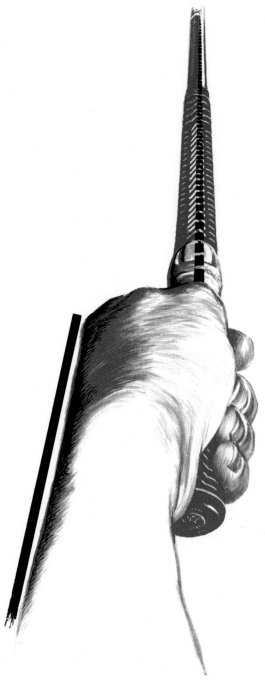

**IDEAL
SQUARE-TO-SQUARE GRIP**

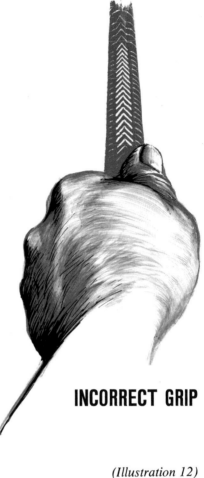

INCORRECT GRIP

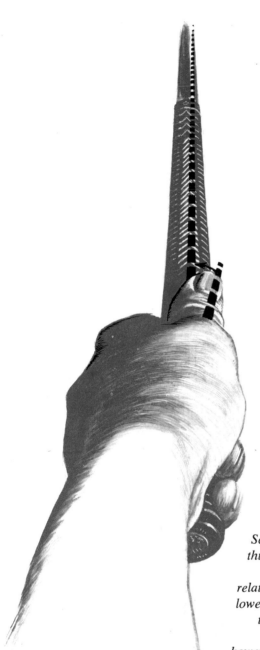

RECOMMENDED
"FIRST STEP" GRIP

(Illustration 12)
"Ideal" left-hand grip for making a Square-to-Square swing (far-left drawing) has thumb directly on top of clubshaft. Such a grip establishes from the start a straight-line relationship between back of the hand, wrist and lower forearm — the so-called "square" position that is required during impact to consistently square clubface to the target line. At first, however, most golfers switching to the Square-to-Square Method will lack sufficient strength in their left hand, arm and side to employ this ideal grip. They are advised to assume the "first-step" grip, with thumb resting slightly to top-right of shaft (near-left drawing), and then move into "square" position during takeaway. Such players can change to the ideal grip as left-side strength develops. Incorrect grip should be avoided.

a manner at this point. Most golfers simply lack the *strength* in their left arm and hand to start from this position and maintain it throughout the swing.

"Strength?" you might ask. "Who needs strength? Why, the heaviest club in my bag weighs barely a pound!"

The golf swing, *if properly executed,* is as much an athletic act as kicking a football or hurling a baseball. It requires coordination *and* strength. If you doubt the need for strength in the golf swing, merely grip a driver solely in your left hand as we have described— back of left hand, wrist and lower forearm forming a straight line and facing square to the target line. With your left arm fully extended, move the club up to the top of your swing. Check that at the top of your swing your arm is still extended, and that the back of your hand, wrist and lower forearm still forms a straight line. If you have made a full backswing, you should find it almost impossible physically to hold this proper top-of-swing position for more than a few seconds, if that long.

To be sure, when making an actual swing your right hand will also be on the club. However, *the degree of success you achieve with the Square-to-Square Method will be determined largely by the degree to which you minimize the control of the club by your right hand, arm and side. The more dominant you make your left-side control, the straighter you will hit your shots.*

Therefore, although the "square-to-target" grip with the left hand is ideal, most golfers should move towards this ideal grip gradually, as they develop their left-side muscles.

Those who teach Square-to-Square would rather see newcomers to the Method grip with their left hand so that the thumb rests slightly to the top-right of the shaft *(illustration 12),* rather than directly on top, while holding the club slightly more in the fingers than in the palm. The clubshaft should be positioned so that the last three fingers wedge it against the meaty pad at the heel of the palm.

As you progress with the Method, you can gradually position your left hand so that it is turned more and more to the left, until

LEFT-SIDE STRENGTH

(Illustration 13)
*Swinging a golf club properly requires more strength than
most golfers realize. To achieve maximum success with
the Square-to-Square Method, the golfer must develop
and train his or her normally weaker left hand, arm
and side to dominate. Try making a full backswing with
only the left hand holding the club and with the left arm
remaining straight. As you hold your top-of-the-swing
position, you will realize that the proper swing is a highly
physical act. The fact that touring professionals have
developed their left-side muscles to a high degree —
and learned to subordinate right-side muscles—through
years of playing and practicing is one major reason
why they achieve such amazing distance and
accuracy on their shots.*

eventually your left thumb is on top of the shaft and the back of
your hand faces down the target line. By moving towards the ideal
left-hand grip gradually, you will also minimize the feeling of strange-
ness that occurs at first with almost any grip change.

As for the right hand, it should always be facing the left—palm
parallel to palm—with the club being held almost entirely in the
fingers *(illustration 14)*.

CHECKPOINT. *Grip the club in what you consider to be proper position. Open your hands and straighten your fingers. Note if your hands are now parallel to each other. If not, retain the left hand in proper position as described above and move right hand into "palms-parallel" position. Re-grip club without any further turning of the hands.*

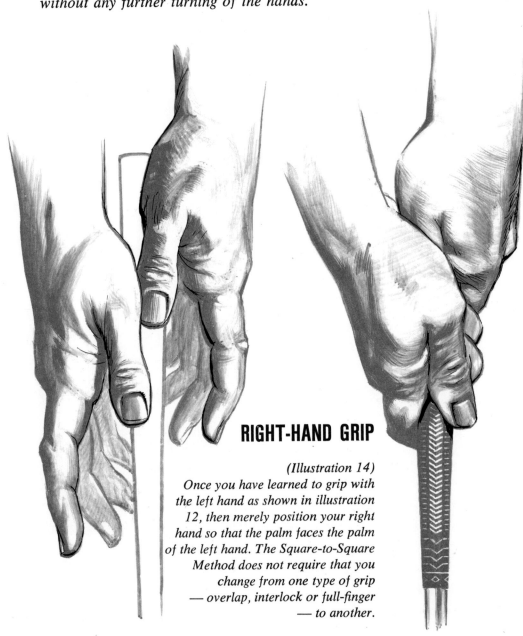

RIGHT-HAND GRIP

(Illustration 14)
Once you have learned to grip with the left hand as shown in illustration 12, then merely position your right hand so that the palm faces the palm of the left hand. The Square-to-Square Method does not require that you change from one type of grip — overlap, interlock or full-finger — to another.

PROPER GRIP PRESSURE

The other goals that we seek to encourage through proper gripping—swinging on a relatively upright plane, keeping the clubface from fanning open, sustaining clubhead speed and avoiding slippage of the club—are largely dependent on grip pressure, rather than on the positioning of the hands.

Teachers of the Method advocate that grip pressure be emphasized in the last three fingers of the left hand. Pressure with the thumb and forefinger of the left hand, and all fingers of the right hand, should be only firm enough to avoid any slippage.

Gripping the club primarily in the last three fingers of the left hand, immediately begins to put your left side in control, by activating the muscles on the underside of your left forearm *(illustration 15)*. With these muscles in charge, the normal tendency is to start the clubhead *straight back from the ball with the clubface continuing to look down the target line*. Starting the clubhead straight back puts the swing on a properly upright plane and also precludes fanning open the clubface. Thus, grip pressure in the last three fingers of the left hand directly influences plane and clubface alignment during the swing.

CHECKPOINT. *If you are properly emphasizing pressure in the last three fingers of your left hand, you should experience a bunching of muscles on the underside of your left forearm, just below the elbow, when you grip with the clubhead resting on the ground. Too much pressure with the thumb and forefinger will reduce this bunching and increase tension in the forearm's upper side.*

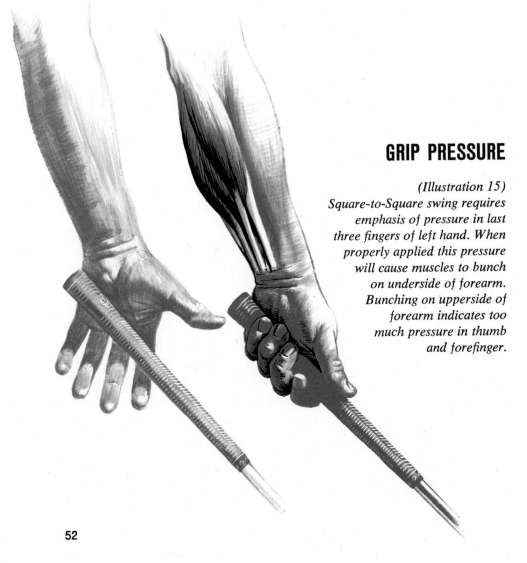

GRIP PRESSURE

(Illustration 15)
Square-to-Square swing requires emphasis of pressure in last three fingers of left hand. When properly applied this pressure will cause muscles to bunch on underside of forearm. Bunching on upperside of forearm indicates too much pressure in thumb and forefinger.

Too much pressure in the grip of the right hand will cause your right arm and shoulder muscles to tighten. Such tightening greatly restricts your ability to make a full shoulder turn on a sufficiently upright plane. Right-hand pressure also causes the right side to take over on the backswing. This causes a premature lifting of the clubhead, which shortens and flattens your swing. Your left side, with the last three fingers of your left hand dominating your grip, should be responsible for moving the clubhead back and up on the backswing.

GRIP SUMMARY

Proper gripping paves the way for relatively easy attainment of certain goals of the Square-to-Square Method. The ideal grip finds the back of the left hand and forearm square to the target line, with the thumb on top of the club, but newcomers to the Method should move gradually towards this positioning as they strengthen their left side. The right hand should be positioned so that when the hands are opened, the palms are exactly parallel to each other.

Grip pressure should be emphasized in the last three fingers of the left hand. The muscles of the underside of the left arm, as opposed to those of the upperside, should be taut. The thumb and forefinger of the left hand, and all fingers of the right hand, should grip only firmly enough to hold onto the club.

CHAPTER
THREE

SETTING UP FOR
A SQUARE-TO-SQUARE SWING

A ny golfer who hopes to become proficient at the game must learn
first how to stand up to the ball properly. Both those professionals
who teach the Square-to-Square swing and those who do not agree
that proper address position is basic to a successful swing. If you
don't "set up" properly, you will never become a low-handicap golfer,
they say. A proper address position is as vital in making a good golf
swing as is the steering wheel in directing an automobile.

The reason that the way you set up to the ball is so important
to the direction and distance of your shots is because *the alignment
and posture of your body at address directly determines how you
will swing the club.*

Try standing up to an imaginary golf ball with an imaginary
club in your hand. Instead of bending at your knees and your waist,

however, stand perfectly upright. Obviously, this is no way to address a golf ball, but we are creating an extreme situation to prove a point —that address position does, indeed, influence the swing itself.

Now from your upright address position move your hands back and up as you would during your backswing, but don't allow any bending at the knees or waist.

Most golfers will find it extremely difficult to move their hands into normal top-of-swing position. The shoulders will not turn as fully as they should—your left shoulder probably will bump your chin. The tendency will be to move your hands *around*—as if swinging at a baseball pitch—rather than *up and around,* as is normal for the golf swing.

This exercise, as noted, involves an address position that obviously is extremely faulty. It is safe to say, however, that, to a lesser degree, hundreds of thousands of the world's golfers do not bend *quite* enough from the waist. Because of insufficient or improper bending from the waist they do not turn their shoulders on a plane that is *quite* sufficiently upright, or tilted—not enough like a Ferris wheel, or too much like a merry-go round. Hence, they do not strike the ball as powerfully or as consistently straight as they could.

Other failures at address will bring forth other flaws in the swing. The golfer who sets up improperly must necessarily invoke compensations during his swing. The more compensations in the swing, the less chance for a "perfect" shot—a shot made with club-head facing down target line and moving along that line at maximum speed during impact.

GOALS OF THE ADDRESS POSITION

If we may assume for the moment that the reader realizes the importance of aiming correctly through proper alignment of his clubface, feet, hips and shoulders at address, let us now look at four Square-to-Square swing goals that correctly setting up to the ball will help achieve.

First, your address position must provide a solid base so that you can stay in balance while you swing the club. If you lose some of your balance—if, say, you sway laterally to your right during your backswing—your body will find it necessary to use some of its energy to bring you back into balance. This wastes energy that could be better used to generate clubhead speed. Also, a loss of balance usually throws the swing out of its proper arc and plane and thwarts proper timing. Thus, an address position that allows you to stay in balance—in control of your physical self while swinging—is necessary if you are to consistently strike the ball squarely with maximum clubhead speed.

Second, a sound address position will allow you to swing the club on a sufficiently upright plane to maintain, with *relative* ease, the "square impact" relationship—back of left hand, wrist and lower forearm in straight alignment and parallel to the clubface—throughout the swing.

If your swing plane is sufficiently upright—if your hands move high over your shoulders during your backswing—your shoulders and your left arm, as well as your left thumb and the heel of your left palm, all will be more or less "under" your hands, giving support to the left arm-hand relationship at the top of the swing *(illustration 16)*. If your swing is too flat—if your hands move around "behind" your body—you will not have this support "under" your hands. Your straight-line "square impact" relationship will start to weaken, causing you to unconsciously rush your downswing. As a result, your right hand and side will take over control of the club.

When the right side takes over at the start of the downswing, several negative factors occur to thwart good shotmaking. The club-head tends to be thrown onto a plane that moves it into the ball from outside the target line, causing you to either slice or pull the shot. The straight-line, square impact relationship between the back of the left hand, wrist and lower forearm with the clubface breaks down, causing the left wrist to bend inward. This inward bending closes the clubface and causes off-line shots. The collapsing of the left wrist also causes a "power leak" in the flow of energy from the big body and leg muscles to the clubhead. The weaker arm muscles take over from the stronger leg and back muscles.

Those who teach the Square-to-Square swing advocate an address position that not only produces balance during the swing, as well as a sufficiently upright swing plane, but one that also encourages a third swing goal—a *full* shoulder turn and a *minimal* hip turn. These teachers note that the modern trend toward fuller shoulder turn and lesser hip turn better utilizes the tremendous potential power of the body's big muscles than does the older method of turning the shoulders and hips to more or less the same degree. The combination of big shoulder turn and small hip turn means more distance because it produces more torque. The golfer coils his upper body, as if tightening a coil-spring, against the resistance of his lower body.

Another reason for restricting hip turn is because excessive swiveling of the hips tends to cause the shoulders and upper body to also swivel. This forces the club to be swung on a much flatter plane than is desirable.

But, say those who teach the Square-to-Square Method, "set up to the ball properly and this variance in degree of shoulder and hip turn will happen *automatically*. Address the ball correctly, and you can forget about *consciously* making a big shoulder turn and a small hip turn." *(See illustration 17.)*

The fourth goal of the address position is to set the golfer up so that his lower body—legs

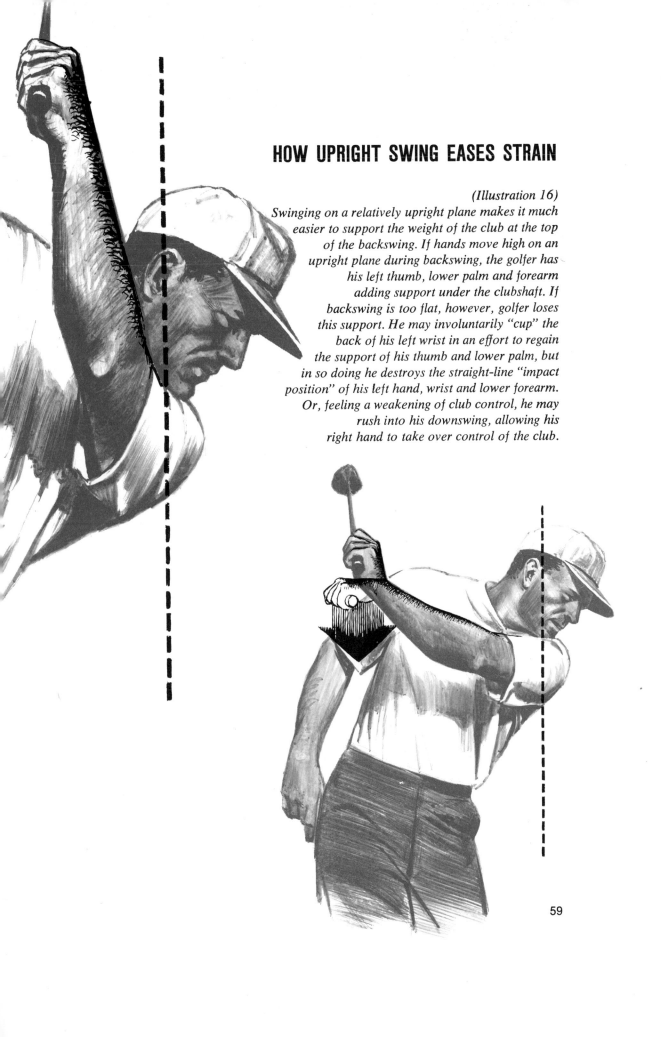

HOW UPRIGHT SWING EASES STRAIN

(Illustration 16)
Swinging on a relatively upright plane makes it much easier to support the weight of the club at the top of the backswing. If hands move high on an upright plane during backswing, the golfer has his left thumb, lower palm and forearm adding support under the clubshaft. If backswing is too flat, however, golfer loses this support. He may involuntarily "cup" the back of his left wrist in an effort to regain the support of his thumb and lower palm, but in so doing he destroys the straight-line "impact position" of his left hand, wrist and lower forearm. Or, feeling a weakening of club control, he may rush into his downswing, allowing his right hand to take over control of the club.

59

CORRECT POSTURE

HOW POSTURE AT ADDRESS AFFECTS YOUR SWING

(Illustration 17)
Proper address posture for Square-to-Square swing emphasizes bending from the waist with spine straight and shoulders pulled back. This bending has the effect of "separating" upper body from lower body so that shoulders automatically will turn more or less independently of hips. This separation allows golfer to fully activate back and leg muscles during backswing by making a big shoulder turn without increasing hip turn. Proper bending at the waist also tilts upper body forward so that shoulders

and hips—can drive forward on the downswing, leading and clearing the way for the hands and, finally, the clubhead. Though Square-to-Square golfers prefer a minimum of hip turn—as opposed to a full shoulder turn—on the backswing, they stress maximum application of leg power during the downswing. Only by leading the downswing with the lower body can the left side continue to dominate the right side. The lower body must drive forward, and your address position had best be such that it will allow the legs and hips maximum freedom of movement during the downswing.

automatically turn on relatively upright plane.
Insufficient bending from the waist, or failure to keep
back straight (incorrect drawings), forces shoulders to turn
on a relatively flat plane and
encourages hips to turn too fully
with the shoulders.

INCORRECT POSTURE   **INCORRECT POSTURE**

HOW TO ADDRESS THE BALL

Thus, we have described the four swing goals that setting up to the ball properly will help achieve. Again, these goals are to swing (1) in balance, (2) on a relatively upright plane, (3) with maximum shoulder turn and minimum hip turn, and (4) with the lower body leading the downswing.

Moving into the proper address position is a four-step procedure. First, the golfer grips the club (see Chapter 2 for specifics on gripping).

Second, the golfer places the clubhead behind the ball so that the clubface looks down the intended line of flight. Most better players ascertain this target line while they are standing at about "7 o'clock"—assuming the ball is the center of the clock and the target line runs from "6" to "12" *(illustration 18a)*. The golfer merely steps up and places the clubhead behind the ball so that it is facing "12"—"square" to the target line.

PITFALL. *The fact that the clubface must be positioned behind the ball so that it looks directly down the target line may seem too elementary to merit mention. However, thousands of golfers unconsciously fall prey to clubface mis-alignment. Square-to-Square instructors stress that failure to properly align the clubface at address will almost assuredly bring forth additional faults during the swing. For instance, the golfer who places his clubhead behind the ball in an opened position —looking to the right of the target line—frequently will "fan open" the clubface to an even greater extent during his takeaway. The toe of the clubhead will lead the heel in moving away from the ball, a move that contradicts the Square-to-Square Method. Most golfers have experienced the errant results of a mis-aligned clubface on a two-foot putt. Imagine what happens when similar mis-alignment takes place on a 600-foot drive.*

The third step is placing the feet—assuming the stance. Instructors of Square-to-Square suggest that you position your right foot so that it points straight out—in the direction you will be facing at address *(illustration 18b)*. This makes the foot "square" to the target line.

Positioning the right foot "square" to the target line will help you achieve one of the aforementioned goals—a minimum hip turn during the backswing. If you were to toe out the right foot so that it pointed to, say, "4 o'clock," you would find it natural to make a fuller hip turn, because the foot would be less likely to resist such turning.

A few golfers—Chi Chi Rodriguez for one—actually toe-in the right foot to further restrict the hip turn. Those who teach the Square-to-Square swing advise against such positioning for most golfers, noting that it could cause a lateral swaying to the right and a loss of balance during the backswing.

The left foot should toe-out slightly—a bit to the left—so that

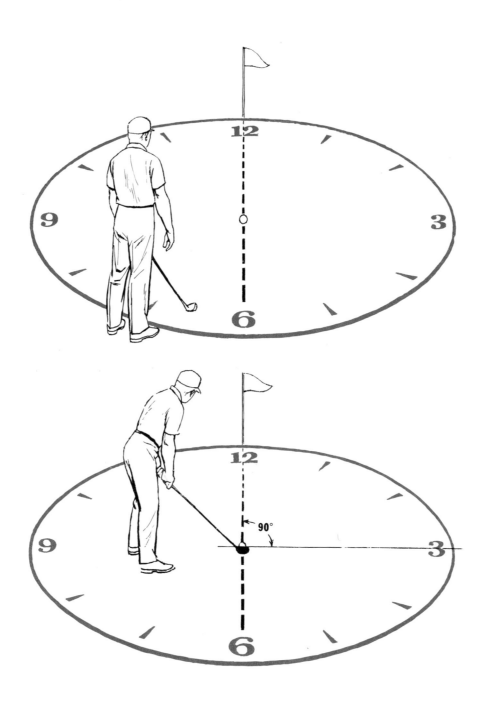

(Illustration 18a)

Most better golfers sight the intended line of flight while standing at approximately "7 o'clock" as shown above. Then they place the clubhead behind the ball so that it faces down the target line—towards "12 o'clock"—before they settle into a proper stance (see illustration 18b).

it points to about "2 o'clock" *(illustration 18b)*.

Toeing-out the left foot will make it easier for you to drive forward with your legs and lower body as they lead the downswing. This vital goal of the Method would be difficult to achieve if the left foot were "square" or toed-in, because such alignment would restrict downswing movement of the legs and lower body, in the same way

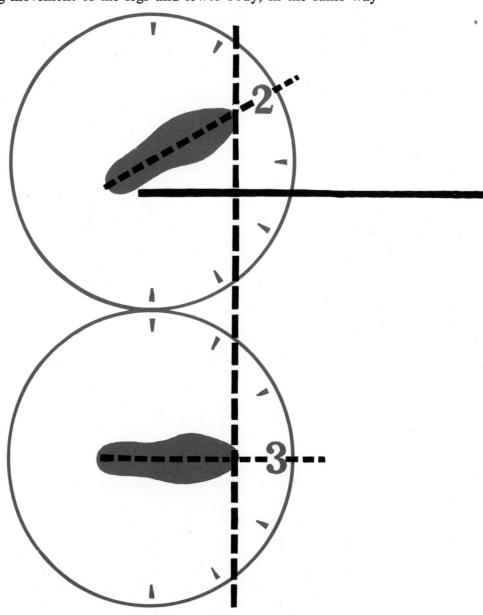

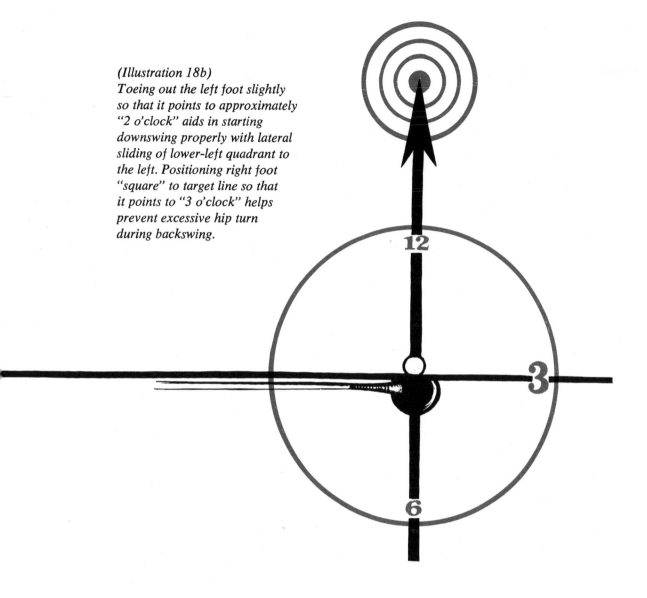

(Illustration 18b)
Toeing out the left foot slightly so that it points to approximately "2 o'clock" aids in starting downswing properly with lateral sliding of lower-left quadrant to the left. Positioning right foot "square" to target line so that it points to "3 o'clock" helps prevent excessive hip turn during backswing.

that the hip turn is restricted on the backswing when the right foot is "square" or toed-in.

As a general rule, the more you toe-out a foot, the easier it will be to turn and move your lower body in the direction you are toeing-out.

Those who teach the Square-to-Square Method advocate the standard "square" stance for most pupils. In this stance an imaginary line across the back of the heels is parallel to the target line. Most professional instructors feel that this foot alignment gives most golfers the best chance to pull the clubhead along the target line in returning it to the ball.

Some players who employ the Square-to-Square Method—Jack Nicklaus for one—prefer a slightly "open" foot alignment. In such a stance the left foot is not only toed-out slightly, but also the right foot is positioned forward, a bit closer than the left foot to the target line. An imaginary line across the heels of an "open" stance points to the left of target. The golfer who can stand slightly "open," yet still swing the clubhead along the target line during impact, will find it possible to pull his legs and lower body through with maximum ease and force during his downswing.

Most Square-to-Square teachers encourage golfers to *evolve* from a square stance to a slightly open stance if those golfers can still swing the clubhead *along* the target line during impact. They also encourage such players to seek additional lower-body thrust by allowing their hips to also evolve to a slightly open position as they gradually open their stance.

An open stance and open hip positioning not only encourages lower-body thrust during the downswing, but such positioning also helps the golfer achieve the Square-to-Square goal of minimal hip turning during the backswing.

However, almost all who teach the Method advocate positioning the shoulders "square" at address, so that a line across the shoulders is parallel to the target line. Since it is natural to take the club back from the ball along an extension of the shoulder line, "square" shoulder alignment facilitates a straight-back takeaway and a sufficiently upright swing plane. Also, an "open" shoulder position at address would make it unnecessarily difficult to achieve a full shoulder turn on the backswing. Thus an open shoulder position would tend to unnecessarily minimize the disparity between minimal hip turn and maximum shoulder turn that is needed to fully stretch the big muscles during the backswing.

Instructors of the Method suggest that most weight be placed on the left foot at address. This tends to make the shoulders turn more fully on a relatively upright plane. Such weight distribution also minimizes hip turning and makes it easier to avoid shifting weight onto the outside of the right foot during the backswing. Further restricting the hip turn in this manner adds to a build-up of tension in the legs during the backswing—tension in the form of additional clubhead speed if the downswing begins correctly.

Square-to-Square instructors feel that a golfer's *posture* at address has as much to do with influencing the success or failure of his swing as does his stance and hip and shoulder alignment. Assuming proper posture is the fourth step in setting up to the ball.

Here is a good way to assume the address position posture that best serves those who seek to swing according to the Square-to-Square Method *(see illustrations 19a, 19b and 19c)*.

First, position your feet as suggested in earlier paragraphs.

Next, keeping the feet in position, pull yourself up to "attention," as you would if you were in the army. Make sure that your hands are at your sides, eyes forward, shoulders back, chest out, and stomach pulled in. Actually, "suck in" the stomach.

Next, while maintaining this position of "attention," bend slightly at your knees, as if you were starting to sit, until you feel tension in the upper part of your thighs.

Then, with your upper body still at "attention," bend forward *from the waist*. Keep your shoulders back and your stomach in.

> CHECKPOINT. *If you have followed this procedure correctly to this point, you should sense a "hollow" or "concave" feeling in the small of your back. If you do not experience this sensation, you probably are allowing your spine to curve. Try the procedure again, this time stressing "stomach in," "shoulders back," and bending "from the waist."*

Finally, move your hands forward and grip an imaginary club. Your left arm should be fully extended. The right arm should be slightly bent and should feel relaxed. Many instructors add that Square-to-Square goals will be best served if the golfer holds the club with his hands sufficiently forward—toward the target—so that his left arm and clubshaft form a continuous line.

CHECKPOINT. *If you have bent forward from the waist a sufficient amount, your hands should come together under your upper-chest, so that you would be forced to look down and back, as opposed to down and out, to see your hands. Imagine a vertical line from your eyes to the ground. If any part of your hands are positioned out beyond this line, you are reaching too much with your arms. In that case, bring your hands closer to your body by pushing downward with your thumbs and pulling your arms in toward you. As you push down with your thumbs, you will note a raising of the wrists. If your hands are now "inside" the vertical line from your eyes, you are in proper address position.*

Practice assuming your address position several times, preferably in front of a mirror,

HOW TO ASSUME PROPER POSTURE

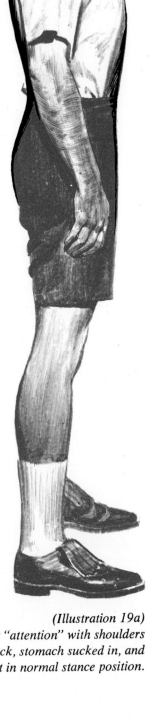

(Illustration 19a)
1. *Stand at "attention" with shoulders pulled back, stomach sucked in, and feet in normal stance position.*

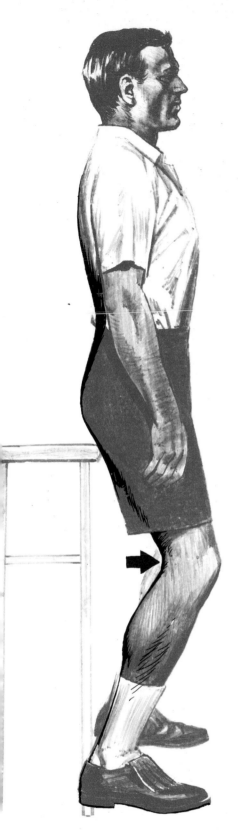

(Illustration 19b)
2. *Without any bending—spine still at "attention"— flex knees slightly as if starting to sit.*

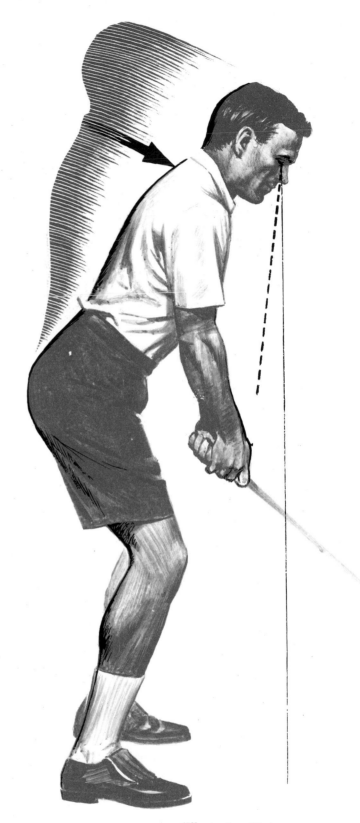

(Illustration 19c)
3. *Bend forward from waist. If back is still straight and shoulders pulled back, rear end should protrude. Lower back should feel "hollow." Viewing hands should require "looking back."*

until you feel you have it right. Then try doing it with a golf club in your hands.

It would be wise at this point for you to read over the summary on proper gripping (chapter 2). Be especially careful that your right-hand grip is no firmer than is necessary to hold onto the club while swinging. If you grip the club properly and assume your address position correctly, you should feel absolutely no tension in your right hand, arm or shoulder. The right arm should hang "easy," ready to *be moved* by the firmer left side on the backswing.

It is absolutely vital to the Square-to-Square Method that your right hand, arm and shoulder be relaxed at address. Only when the right side is submissive to the left can you make a full shoulder turn on a sufficiently upright plane during your backswing *(illustration 20)*. Tension in the upper-right "quadrant" during your backswing will restrict such a turn and cause your swing plane to flatten. Also, because right-side tension reduces left-side dominance, this strong right-side will make it more difficult for you to maintain the straight-line relationship between the back of the left hand, wrist and lower forearm that is so basic in the Square-to-Square swing.

ADDITIONAL ADDRESS POSITION CHECKPOINTS

Most golfers probably will find that the address position described in this chapter feels "different." This is to be expected.

Your back may feel and look straighter with less bend at your neck. It *should* be straighter, especially if your shoulders are still pulled back.

You should feel that your rear end is protruding, and your legs should feel springy, with your weight on your left foot and the inner part of your right. If you take a few practice swings, you may note that you do not achieve quite as much hip turn as you once did.

You probably will feel that your head and shoulders are more "over" the ball because of increased bending at the waist. Remember that you should be able to "look back" at your hands. You may find that your clubhead positions itself closer to your feet than before.

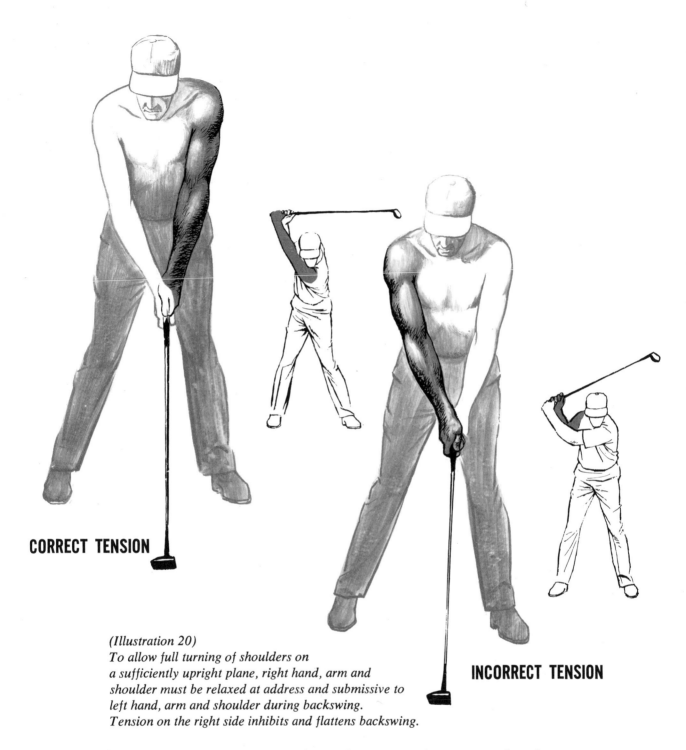

CORRECT TENSION

INCORRECT TENSION

(Illustration 20)
To allow full turning of shoulders on
a sufficiently upright plane, right hand, arm and
shoulder must be relaxed at address and submissive to
left hand, arm and shoulder during backswing.
Tension on the right side inhibits and flattens backswing.

As you take some practice swings, you also may notice that your shoulders now turn on a more vertical or upright plane, more like a Ferris wheel than a merry-go-round. Your left shoulder may be moving more down and under your chin—and with greater ease

—during your backswing. Your hands may be moving higher on your backswing.

All of these sensations are normal. You may even feel uncomfortable—tight and cramped. Probably, at first, you will have difficulty striking shots squarely when you employ this new address position.

But don't be discouraged, even if it takes you several practice sessions before things begin feeling normal. *Make up your mind to refuse to compensate for unsual sensations by returning to old habits.* Accept the fact that you are learning a new method—that you are making several changes in your grip and address position—and that these changes are bound to cause some discomfort.

Periodically re-check this text and compare the instructions and illustrations herein with your own grip and address position. If your posture and stance do look and feel like the text describes they should, you will indeed be properly positioned to achieve those goals mentioned earlier in this chapter. You will be ready to swing in balance, on a relatively upright plane, with a full shoulder turn and minimal hip turn, and with strong leg and lower-body action on the downswing.

SUMMARY

Address position directly affects your swing. Only a proper address position will keep compensatory moves during the swing to a minimum.

The advocated address position enables golfers to more readily —almost automatically in some cases—achieve certain swing goals that are required by the Square-to-Square Method. These goals include swinging in good balance, swinging on a relatively upright plane, making a full shoulder turn and minimal hip turn, and leading the downswing with a dynamic pulling of the legs and lower body.

The proper stance to achieve these goals has the right foot positioned "square" to the target line, with the left foot toed-out slightly. The foot and hip alignment should be square or slightly open. The shoulder alignment should be square.

The proper posture for achieving these goals finds the legs feeling springy, with a slight bend at the knees and the weight primarily on the left foot. The back should be straight and feel concave in its lower portion. The stomach should be pulled in and the shoulders back. The rear end should protrude. The hands should be "inside" a vertical line from the eyes. The left hand should be gripping firmly in the last three fingers and the left arm should be extended in line with the clubshaft. The right hand, arm and shoulder should feel free of tension.

CHAPTER
FOUR

THE SQUARE-TO-SQUARE BACKSWING

In many ways swinging a golf club is like baking a cake. Those who teach the Square-to-Square Method would point out that gripping the club (chapter 2) and setting up to the ball (chapter 3) are comparable to gathering and measuring the ingredients for the cake. As in cake-baking, if you have the right ingredients of grip and address position you are well along towards making—or "baking"—a super golf swing.

If the grip and address position are comparable to gathering and measuring ingredients for a cake, then the backswing is similar to the process of *blending* the eggs, flour, sugar, etc. As everyone knows, once the proper ingredients are properly measured and properly blended, there is little left to cake-baking. So it is in swinging a golf club. Once you have a proper grip and address position, and once you make a proper backswing, everything else occurs more or less automatically. You merely "turn on the oven" at the start of your downswing.

GOALS OF THE BACKSWING

This chapter will tell how those who teach the Square-to-Square Method advocate "blending" the ingredients of proper grip and set-up into a nice smooth "batter" during the backswing.

The goals of proper address positioning, you will recall, are to (1) provide a base for swinging in good balance, (2) provide a posture that will encourage the shoulders to turn on a sufficiently upright plane, (3) relax the right arm and shoulder area to allow the upper body to coil much more fully than the lower body, and (4) provide correct alignment of feet and hips so that the lower body will lead the downswing with a dynamic pulling action.

The goals of the proper backswing are the same as goals 2 and 3 of the above—to produce a much fuller coiling of the upper body in relation to the lower body, and to turn the upper body on a sufficiently upright plane. (Goals 1 and 4 of the above were achieved during the address procedure and can be put aside for the moment.)

There are, however, two other goals to be achieved during the backswing. The first of these is to further establish left-side dominance. The second additional goal is to move the left hand, wrist and lower forearm into the straight-line "square" position, thereafter to be maintained through impact.

Those who teach the Square-to-Square Method regard left-side dominance as being paramount to success. The left hand, arm and shoulder area must control the club throughout the swing.

If you followed the rules for proper grip and set-up in chapters 2 and 3, you have already provided for some left-side dominance by gripping firmly with the last three fingers of the left hand while keeping the right hand, arm and shoulder area relatively relaxed.

Several things—all bad—will occur if the right side is allowed to assert itself. Right-side dominance will cause you to lift the club too abruptly during the backswing. It will cause you to move the club "around" your body on too flat a swing plane. It will cause your left wrist to weaken and collapse at the top of the backswing, thus destroying the straight-line square relationship between left hand, wrist and lower forearm that you must retain if you are to strike the ball with a "square" clubface.

Right-side dominance also will cause you to rush into your downswing and release the power of your swing prematurely, before your clubhead reaches the ball. Also, your clubhead will not be moving along the target line during impact, nor will it be facing down that line.

The second new goal of the backswing is to establish the straight-line square relationship of left hand, wrist and lower forearm. The back of the hand and the back of the lower forearm must be made continuous, with no break at the wrist. This is the hand-arm relationship that duplicates *in advance* the square position that all golfers should seek to achieve during impact—that is, with the back of the left hand and the lower forearm "square" to the target line.

You will recall earlier mention that, until the era of the steel shaft, golfers sought to move into a square impact position during the downswing by manipulating the club with their hands and arms.

More recently top players—Ben Hogan is the best example—established their impact position at the start of their downswing, moving from a straight or slightly concave back-of-left-wrist position to a straight or slightly convex position, while admirably retaining power by pulling with the legs and lower-left side. This technique does, however, necessitate a flattening of the swing plane when the golfer shifts gears from backswing to downswing.

The Square-to-Square Method allows golfers to move into a square impact position during the slower-moving backswing when they have achieved maximum control of the club. By moving into impact position at this earlier stage, the golfer then can apply the big muscles of the body and legs to their fullest during the downswing, without any further concern about establishing square impact position with the hands and clubhead. You can "let 'er rip," so to speak.

Thus, the proper Square-to-Square backswing not only further establishes the goals of upright swing plane and full upper-body coiling, but also blends in additional emphasis of left-side dominance and puts the left hand, wrist and lower forearm into impact position.

HOW TO MAKE THE BACKSWING

Those who teach the Square-to-Square Method stress over and over to their pupils that the proper backswing will *not* feel natural while they are learning the Method. The reason why this correct backswing feels unnatural is simply because the normally *weaker* left side must dominate the normally *stronger* right side from waggle through impact.

> PITFALL. *Most golfers who adopt the Square-to-Square Method of swinging will experience muscle soreness for a few weeks during the process of changing from right-side to left-side dominance. This is natural and should be expected; you are using "new" muscles, muscles that have been subordinate in the past. Also, you will be stretching certain back and leg muscles more than you did during previous swinging. It is natural that your body will be "resentful" of this increased tension. In fact, some who preach the Method state flatly that pupils who do not experience some discomfort are not executing the Square-to-Square backswing properly.*

One reason for pointing out that the proper backswing will feel unnatural at first, and for some time to come, is to encourage pupils to continue to pursue the Square-to-Square Method despite any immediate discomfort. Look on the soreness and unnatural feeling of the backswing as being exactly what they are—the results of employing new muscles and new tensions to control the club.

> PITFALL. *Not only will newcomers to the Method feel unnatural and physically uncomfortable, but, quite probably, they also will miss-hit more shots than normal. Don't be disappointed if you fail to make solid contact with the ball on many of your shots. It takes time for the senses to become accustomed to holding the club and setting up to the ball in a new and different fashion.*

PITFALL. *Another common pitfall in moving to Square-to-Square is that you may lose some sense of rhythm in swinging. During the backswing you will be mentally directing certain movement. It is inevitable that natural rhythm will suffer when the mind interferes.*

Bear in mind, however, that as the Square-to-Square Method of gripping, setting up and swinging becomes more natural through practice—and as you begin to strengthen the "new" muscles of your left side (or the right side for left-handers)—you will gradually regain your old rhythm as well as new, and far superior, shotmaking skill. The more you strengthen your left side and "teach" it to dominate your right side, the more you will improve. The professional golfer who plays the game for a living has, consciously or unconsciously, developed his or her left side to an extremely high degree through years of striking golf balls. The more you develop your golfing muscles the closer you will come to improving your proficiency. The final chapter in this book details how to develop your left side and should be studied by all who seek dramatic improvement.

HOW TO SWING BACK

A very important move of the swing, according to those who teach the Square-to-Square Method, occurs at the very start of the backswing. This is the move that establishes the straight-line, "square" relationship between the back of the left hand, wrist and lower forearm. It is this movement of the backswing that, once and for all, puts your left hand and arm into the ideal "impact" position. *Once this proper positioning of left hand and forearm is established during the takeaway, and maintained during the swing by a dominant left side, no further manipulation of the hands is necessary to return the clubface squarely to the ball.*

Those who teach the Method describe this vital, first move of the backswing as a *slight* "curling under" of the last three fingers of the left hand *(illustration 21)*. Nothing more. There is no turning of the whole arm involved in this initial move. Only the last three fingers "curl under." This curling under occurs at the very start of the back-swing, just as the clubhead moves back from the ball. *The movement is almost imperceptible. It is not advised for Stage I golfers unless supervised by a competent professional.*

To get an idea of how this move looks and feels, merely put your left hand out in front of you in the same position it would be in if you were gripping a golf club. Hold this imaginary club very gently.

Now squeeze the "club" with the last three fingers. As you squeeze you will notice that these fingers want to "curl under." Let them. As you squeeze and as these fingers curl under, you will gradually see less and less of the back of your hand. *Continue the curling under only until the back of your hand and the back of your forearm form a straight line.*

Practice this move a few times until the curling under and squeezing of the last three fingers feels natural. You should feel a bunching of muscles on the *underside* of your forearm.

For golfers who grip the club with the back of their left hand already "square" to the target line—back of hand facing down target line—this "curling under" will be more of a "feeling" than an actual movement—just enough to overcome inertia and establish dominance in their left hand and arm. Those golfers who grip with the left hand slightly "on top" of the clubshaft—back of the hand facing slightly upward—will need to actually curl under, but just enough to straighten the line formed by the back of the hand and the back of the lower forearm. The more the back of your hand faces upward— as opposed to toward the target—in your grip, the more you must curl under during your takeaway. However, any golfer whose left-hand grip is proper, as described in Chapter 2, will find that the amount of curling under needed to straighten the hand-arm relationship is minimal, all but imperceptible.

Some of those who teach the Square-to-Square swing, such as Bill Strausbaugh, 1966 PGA Professional of the Year, and a dominant figure in the Square-to-Square movement, actually encourage

MOVING INTO THE SQUARE POSITION

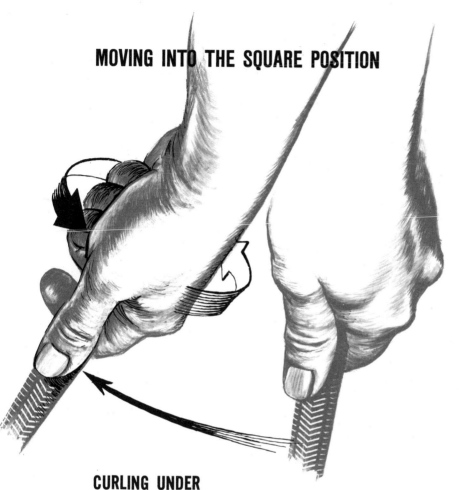

CURLING UNDER

(Illustration 21)

*A slight "curling under" with the
last three fingers of the left hand while
the clubhead moves straight back from the ball
not only helps establish left-side dominance, but
also puts the back of the left hand, wrist
and lower forearm into the vital straight-line,
"square" impact" position at a time when the
golfer has maximum control of his or
her swing. Once this square position
is established, the player must merely
maintain it through impact to
assure that clubface will be square
to the target line when it strikes the ball.
The curling-under, accentuated here and shown
from two different perspectives, should be slight—
merely enough to establish straight-line position.*

pupils to practice the curling under movement as a separate part of the backswing. They ask the student, during practice sessions, to curl under, then pause, and then continue the backswing.

"Some of my pupils make better shots when they practice with this pause than they do when they actually make a continuous backswing," Strausbaugh notes.

While the main purpose of curling under with the last three fingers is to establish the back of the left hand, wrist and lower forearm in the straight-line position, the movement also performs other functions vital to the Square-to-Square Method.

First, curling under further establishes that the left hand dominate the right in controlling the club. This dominance, once established by applying pressure in the last three fingers while gripping and by curling under during the takeaway, must continue throughout the swing.

Second, curling under with the last three fingers also encourages the left shoulder to start to lower, or tilt downward, during the backswing. Readers will recall that turning the shoulders on a tilted plane that is relatively upright—as opposed to flat or horizontal—is a major goal of the backswing.

Third, curling under tends to eliminate any looseness or flippiness of the wrists that may be occurring at the top of your backswing, thus increasing club control at a crucial point in the swing.

As soon as you feel you have mastered the curling under movement, you will be ready to incorporate it into your backswing—and even into your waggle. Most good golfers waggle the clubhead before swinging by moving it backward and forward *behind* the ball. In so doing they more or less preview their takeaway movement. Less-skilled players waggle the clubhead *forward* of the ball; using largely the right hand, or they lift the club up and down over the ball. Waggling behind the ball does allow you to practice the curling-under movement before you actually start to swing. Waggling in this manner—squeezing and curling under the last three fingers of the left hand—gradually will help strengthen your left side control, while also serving to reduce tension in your right hand and arm.

WON'T CURLING UNDER "CLOSE" CLUBFACE?

At this point it is necessary to discuss briefly a common misunderstanding regarding the Square-to-Square Method, that being the fear —especially among low handicap players—that curling under during the takeaway will "close" the clubface and thus promote hooking; a "problem," incidentally, that many chronic slicers wish they had.

It is true that curling under does tend to "close" the clubface, if one accepts the common usage of the term "close." It does not, however, promote hooking. Square-to-Square Method teachers might explain it this way:

For years the accepted swing method has been the so-called "one-piece" swing. This method is still employed by many of the top players. Those who teach the Square-to-Square swing look on it with favor for those pupils who lack the strength, experience or ambition to master Square-to-Square.

The one-piece swing is so-called because it stresses the importance of eliminating any independent turning of the hands during the backswing—no fanning open of the clubface with a clockwise turning of the hands and no curling under with a counterclockwise turning. The golfer merely swings the club back with all parts moving as a unit—in "one piece."

Unfortunately, there is one problem that the one-piece backswing fails to solve. To illustrate this problem merely take a club—preferably a long-iron—and align the leading edge of the clubface with some clearly defined, straight-line object, such as a door jamb or the separation line between linoleum squares, as you assume your address position. Next, without moving the clubhead, laterally slide your hips and hands to your left, into proper impact position—with your hands ahead of the clubface and no inward bending at the back of your left wrist. As you make this shift from address to impact position, you will note a slight opening of the clubface. It tends to turn to face slightly to the right of where it had been facing during address. Though this opening of the face appears slight, it is sufficient to cause a 200-yard shot to slice 10-30 yards off line.

To offset this tendency of the clubface to open, golfers must make some *counter-opening,* or *"closing,"* movement during their swing, some minor adjustment that will return the clubface to a "square-to-target" alignment during impact.

Since the "one-piece" method disallows any "closing" of the clubface during the backswing, such adjustment must come either at the top of the swing or during the downswing to provide a square clubface at impact. The Square-to-Square Method merely provides this necessary squaring of the clubface during the backswing when the club is moving slowly. This frees the golfer to complete the rest of his or her swing without further adjustment.

As discussed earlier in this series, Square-to-Square instructors regard the practice of designating clubface positioning—"open," "closed," and "square"—as being unreliable indicators of a player's true swinging technique. Therefore they prefer that the slight curling-under movement not be considered a closing of the clubface, but rather the establishment of the straight-line relationship between the back of the left hand, wrist and lower forearm and clubface that is ideal for square alignment during impact. In short, these teachers point out that, by curling under during the takeaway, the golfer is actually moving into his "square" impact relationship. Hence the designation "Square (position during takeaway) to Square (position during impact)."

These instructors further note that while curling under is a definite movement to eliminate any slicing caused by an open clubface at impact, it also prevents hooking due to a closed clubface so long as the golfer's grip is proper and if he establishes and *maintains* the straight-line square position. Should this position collapse, if the back of the left wrist bends inward just before or during impact, naturally the clubface will close.

At the beginning of your actual swing, as you curl under on your takeaway, you should move the clubhead along a path straight back from the ball. Your left arm should be extending fully *(illustration 22)*. If your right hand and right side are sufficiently subordinate and relaxed, you will feel that your left hand and arm are pushing the clubhead back and out along that portion of the target line that continues behind the ball.

If you have curled under properly, your clubface should continue to look at the target—square to the target line—as long as it is moving along that line. There should be no indication that the toe of the clubhead is moving back before the heel. If the toe leads the way back, you have fanned open the clubface. If you find that this is occurring, you must further emphasize curling under, until it seems that the heel of the club is leading the toe going back.

The clubhead should move straight back from the ball until it passes the right foot, and then gradually begin to move inside the target line. Taking the club straight back for this distance serves two vital purposes. First, it assures that you achieve full extension of your left arm. This extension is vital if the left side is to dominate the swing. Should the left arm bend, the right hand will take over control of the club. Second, moving the clubhead straight back for a goodly distance encourages the shoulders to tilt on a sufficiently upright plane. If the clubhead is allowed to move inside the target line and around the body at this stage, the shoulders will turn on too-level a plane.

CHECKPOINT. *Many golfers will feel that as they take the club straight back from the ball they are pushing the clubhead outside, out beyond the target line. Do not be alarmed at this feeling so long as the clubhead does not actually move outside the line. The feeling of "pushing out" is due merely to the fact that heretofore you have been lifting the clubhead with your right hand instead of pushing it back with your left.*

PITFALL. *The one pitfall that some players may experience in taking the club straight back is that they may do so to the*

SQUARE-TO-SQUARE TAKEAWAY

(Illustration 22)
*As you "curl under" with the last three fingers of your left hand
(see illustration 21) you should push the clubhead straight back from
the ball with left arm extending fully. Taking the clubhead
straight back forces your left shoulder to start turning under on
a plane that will help give you a sufficiently upright swing.
If clubhead moves inside target line too soon, swing plane probably
will become too flat. If you curl under properly, and just enough
to establish a straight-line relationship between the back of your
left hand, wrist and lower forearm, your clubface will continue to
look down the target line, with no indication that its toe is
moving back ahead of its heel.*

extent that they sway their upper bodies laterally to the right. If this happens to you, you have not set up to the ball properly. Check to see that you are bent at your waist, with your back straight, to such a degree that you must "look back" to see your hands. The more you bend from the waist with your back straight, the easier it will be to take the club straight back from the ball and to turn your shoulders on a tilted plane. Also, make sure that your right knee remains slightly flexed during your backswing. Should this knee stiffen, your hips will turn too much, your plane will flatten, and your right side will take over during your downswing.

It is the turning of the shoulders on a *tilted* plane that forces the clubhead to begin moving inside the line *and* upward. If the shoulders turned on a level plane, one with no tilt, the clubhead would move inside, around the body, but it would not move upward. It is the *tilting* of the shoulders—lowering of the left shoulder and the resultant raising of the right—that causes the clubhead to move upward. Those instructors who teach the Square-to-Square Method insist that during the backswing the club must be "worked" up by the left shoulder's moving down and under the golfer's chin *(illustration 23)*. The club must not, they stress, be lifted by the hands and arms independently of the shoulder turn. When the club is lifted, the right hand and arm will automatically do much of the lifting. This puts the normally stronger right hand and arm back in control and forces the club to move out of proper plane.

CHECKPOINT. *As you push the clubhead back and up with your left hand and arm, and as your left shoulder begins to work its way down and under your chin, you should gradually experience a definite feeling of increasing tension across your back and down your left side and thigh. This tension is normal. It tells you that you are using the big muscles of your body. You should feel more and more taut as your shoulders continue to turn on their tilted plane and "work" the club up to the top of your backswing.*

PITFALL. *It is absolutely essential that during your backswing your right knee remain slightly bent, just as it was at address. Should this leg straighten during your backswing, your hips will swivel into a much fuller turn than is desirable. Such a full hip turn can force your swing plane to become too level. A good way to guard against straightening your right leg during your backswing is to address the ball with definite downward pressure on the inward part of your right foot. Keep this pressure on this inward portion throughout your backswing.*

FURTHER BACKSWING CHECKPOINTS AND PITFALLS

There are several ways to check to see that you are making a proper backswing. While you are in the learning stages of developing the Square-to-Square Method, it is advisable to make these checks time and again.

First, make sure that you are reaching the square position by curling under slightly the last three fingers of your left hand at the start of your backswing, *without any turning of your left arm.* If you are doing this correctly, and if you are taking the clubhead straight back from the ball, the clubface should continue to look at the target until the clubhead finally begins to move to inside the target line. You should never see the toe of the club move back ahead of the heel.

Here is a further check to see that you are properly establishing and maintaining the straight-line, square relationship with the back of the left hand, wrist and lower forearm. When swinging with a driver, you should lose sight of the face of the club during your takeaway. Thereafter you should never again be able to see the face of the club during your swing, even if you turn your head to look at the clubhead. After the takeaway, you will see a part of the clubface only if you have fanned open the face instead of properly establish-

"WORKING" THE CLUB UP

CORRECT

INCORRECT

(Illustration 23)

If you have worked the club up by turning your shoulders on a tilted plane, the clubshaft should be about vertical and your left arm should be straight at the moment when your hands have reached shoulder height. Working the club up in this manner helps assure that your left side remains in control and that you are fully stretching the big muscles of your back and legs. If you raise the club by merely lifting your hands, without much shoulder-turning, your left arm will bend and your clubshaft will move past vertical by the time your hands reach shoulder height. You will fail to create sufficient tension in your back and leg muscles.

89

ing and maintaining the square position by curling under.

If you face a mirror to check yourself while making your backswing, when your hands have moved to shoulder-height your clubshaft should be more or less vertical—pointing straight up—and your left arm still extended. If your clubshaft has moved beyond vertical—continued on toward horizontal—when your hands are shoulder-high, then you have not extended your left arm fully and you have not properly lowered your left shoulder early in your backswing. Make sure, again, that you are pushing the clubhead out and back along the target line with a fully extended left arm during your takeaway. Make sure that your clubhead is raising as a result of your left shoulder's lowering, and not because you are lifting it with your right hand and arm.

Another checkpoint is to see that your right hand, arm and side feel "soft" throughout your backswing and at the top of your swing. They should feel just as relaxed as they were at the address position.

You also should experience an increasing, downward pressure on the inside—left side—of your right foot as you make your backswing. If you feel this pressure, you are retaining the balance and slight flexing of the knee that you established at address. If this feeling of pressure moves onto the outside of your right foot, you will either sway laterally to the right, or you will make a hip turn that is too large. In either case you will not achieve full use of the big muscles in your back and legs, and you will find it difficult to maintain left-side control.

At the top of your backswing your left wrist should be firm and straight, forming the continuous line between the back of your left hand and lower forearm. Again, this is the "square" position that you must maintain throughout your swing until the ball is well on its way. Check yourself in the mirror to see that you have maintained this relationship (illustration 24).

Also, check in the mirror to see if you can hold this square position momentarily at the top of your swing *with your left arm still extended*. For most golfers this will be quite difficult to do because they lack sufficient strength in their left wrist and arm and side. The longer the shaft of the club you are using, the more of a strain it will be to hold this square position.

To relieve this strain on the left hand, arm and side while swinging, most golfers resort to one or more compensations. Some allow the back of the left wrist to bend inward or "collapse." This forms a slight cupping at the back of the wrist; you will note some wrinkling of the skin at the back of the wrist when this occurs. Others who feel strain at the top of the backswing will allow the left arm to bend, or the left-hand grip to loosen. Another common compensation is to grip tighter with the right hand so that it aids the left hand in supporting the club. All of these compensations bring forth right-side control and must be resisted.

Also, in your first attempts to maintain the square position of the left wrist and to keep the left arm extended at the top of your swing, you may start your downswing too soon. This is a natural reaction when your subconscious realizes that your left hand and arm are weakening and losing control of the club. This lowering of the hands prematurely on the downswing will, indeed, ease the strain on your left hand and arm, but it will, unfortunately, put your right side into the dominant role. You will be foresaking your all-important left-side control.

The reason why golfers fall prey to these compensations at the top of the backswing—and those who teach the Square-to-Square Method readily admit the fact—is that swinging properly does indeed require that the normally weaker left side dominate the normally stronger right side.

Lest golfers throw in the towel at this point and revert to any of the above-mentioned compensations, those who teach the Method emphasize that an upright swing plane will ease greatly the burden placed on the left side.

You will readily appreciate the importance of an upright swing plane if you merely make this quick experiment. First, make a backswing that follows the methods prescribed in this chapter. When you

SQUARE

SQUARE POSITION AT TOP OF SWING

(Illustration 24)
If golfer has worked the club up
on a sufficiently upright plane,
the straight-line relationship
between the back of the left hand, wrist
and lower forearm indicates that he is in the
"square position" at the top of his swing. No further
manipulation of the club will be needed to return it to a square
impact position so long as left side remains in control. When back of
left wrist bends outward (convex) or cups inward (concave), golfer must
compensate on downswing to avoid striking ball with closed or open clubface.

reach the top of your swing, with your left arm still extended and your square hand-arm position still intact, move your hands lower and more behind your back. In other words, place your hands in the position they would be in if you had made an extremely flat backswing.

When your hands are so placed, you will note that it is difficult to maintain control of the club with your left hand and arm. The tendency will be even stronger than before to let the right hand aid the left and thus assume control. The reason for the increased strain is because your hands are no longer over your shoulders so that they can help support your left hand. Also, your thumb is no longer under the clubshaft to further ease the strain.

Now, make a proper backswing, one on which your left shoulder moves down and under and "works" the hands and club into a higher position at the top of your swing. You will find that the more

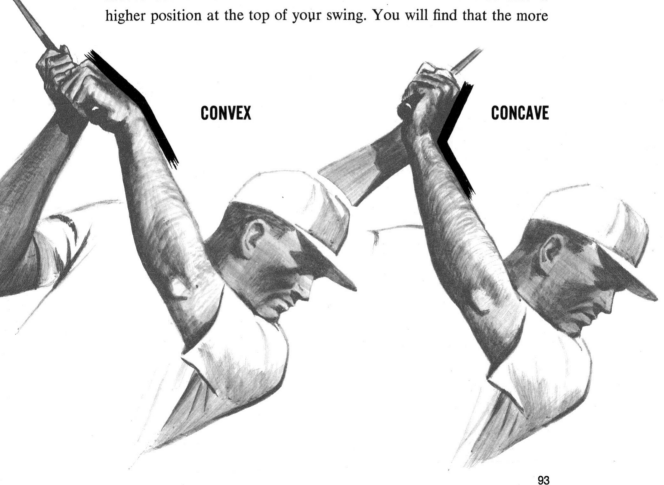

CONVEX CONCAVE

upright swing plane enables you to control the club much more easily with your left hand. In short, though it is possible to establish and maintain left-side control with a relatively flat swing plane, it is possible to do so with less physical effort if you swing on a more upright plane.

Most professional teachers are hesitant to change a golfer's swing plane. They reason that most players have developed a swing plane that feels natural to them, and that they have swung on this plane thousands of times. To suddenly change this ingrained pattern and ask a golfer to swing on a more upright plane would seem comparable to making him switch from driving on the right side of the road to driving on the left.

Those who teach the Square-to-Square Method answer that while most golfers do tend to feel more natural when swinging on a relatively flat swing plane, it *is* possible to alter a golfer's plane—to make it more upright—*without* changing the way the swing *feels*. This alteration of swing plane is made simply by asking the golfer to modify his *address position,* instead of consciously altering the plane of his swing. By modifying the address position, the golfer is made to swing on a more upright plane *automatically,* without any conscious effort on his or her part. By increasing the waist-bend, most golfers will automatically turn their shoulders on a more upright plane. They will be better able to maintain left-side control and the square left hand-arm relationship through the crucial area at the top of the backswing. Obviously, changing one's address position does cause temporary insecurity, but this is readily overcome through practice—in a matter of minutes in most cases.

As they increase their bending from the waist, golfers must consciously avoid the increased tendency to let their back and neck bend and their shoulders to slump forward. Be sure that you retain a hollow, concave feeling in the small of your back, as detailed in Chapter 2.

You can check to see that you have bent sufficiently from the waist to produce a properly upright swing plane by looking at yourself in a full-length mirror. Position yourself as if you were going to hit the ball directly away from the mirror, then make a proper backswing. At the top of your swing, look at yourself in the mirror. It should appear that the angle formed by the edge of your left side and the top of your left thigh is more or less 90 degrees *(illustration 25a)*. If this angle is much greater than 90 degrees, you probably are not bending sufficiently from the waist to produce an upright swing plane. Your shoulders will turn on too-level a plane, too much like a merry-go-round turns. The greater the angle formed by your left side and left thigh, the more horizontal your plane will be *(illustration 25b)*.

While you are checking yourself at this position, you also might note where a line across your shoulders—when fully turned—would point down to the ground. If this line points at the normal ball position, your shoulder turn is truly magnificently upright. Such positioning is the almost "impossible dream" of professional golfers. It is easier to achieve on short iron shots because one stands closer to the ball with the shorter clubs and thus, naturally, turns the shoulders on a more upright plane. Also, it generally is easier for most taller players to achieve a more upright swing plane, again because they must stand closer to the ball to reach it with normal-length clubs.

The next time you go to a professional tournament, stand behind the players—at "6 o'clock"—as they hit practice shots. You will note that, almost without exception, these players are in the square position, with the back of their left hand and forearm straight, at the top of their backswings, and that the angle formed by their left side and thigh is approximately 90 degrees. Thus, these top golfers are, indeed, employing the Square-to-Square swing. They establish the square "impact" position with the back of the left hand and forearm during the backswing while turning their shoulders on a sufficiently tilted plane to maintain this square positioning with relative ease throughout.

Some of these golfers will disclaim, however, that they reach the

TOP-OF-BACKSWING CHECKPOINT

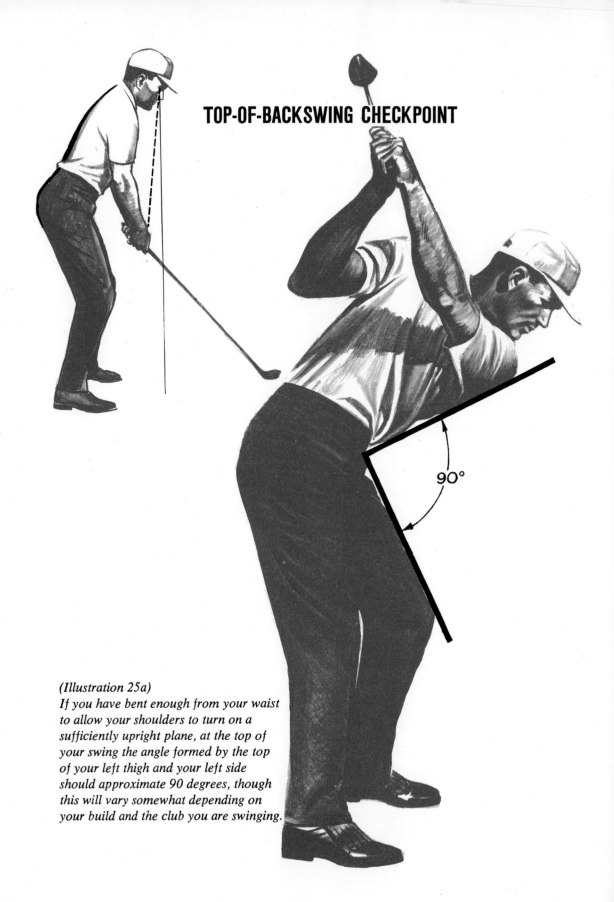

90°

(Illustration 25a)
If you have bent enough from your waist to allow your shoulders to turn on a sufficiently upright plane, at the top of your swing the angle formed by the top of your left thigh and your left side should approximate 90 degrees, though this will vary somewhat depending on your build and the club you are swinging.

(Illustration 25b)
If the angle formed by the top of your left thigh and your left side at the top of your backswing is considerably more than 90 degrees, you probably are not turning your shoulders on a plane that is sufficiently upright to execute the Square-to-Square Method. If such is the case, review your address posture (Chapter 3). Make sure your back is straight and that you are sufficiently bent at waist so that you must "look back" to see your hands.

135°

square position via any "curling under" as described earlier. A few of these players fear that such a move would cause them to reach impact with a closed clubface and thus hook their shots badly. Those who teach the Square-to-Square swing say that this fear is unwarranted, and, as we shall see in the next chapter, firmly maintain that holding the square relationship of left hand and lower forearm through impact is, indeed, a sure way to avoid hooking.

The truth is that most touring professionals grip the club with their left hand and forearm already in the square position. At address their left thumb already is practically on top of the shaft. Thus little curling under is required for them to arrive at the square position during their takeaways. The move is so imperceptible that few of those pros who make the move realize that they do so. The curling-under move is even less noticeable if a golfer moves the clubhead straight back from the ball with left arm fully extended —as practically all of these players do.

However, as mentioned earlier, those who teach the Method advise against most golfers trying to grip with their left thumb directly on top of the shaft, at least until they have firmly established enough strength in their left hand, arm and side to readily sustain the square hand-arm relationship throughout their swings. Gripping with the thumb to top-right of the shaft, and then curling under during the takeaway, helps less-experienced players establish and maintain the square position with less physical effort.

SUMMARY ON THE BACKSWING

The goals of the proper backswing are (1) to establish the "square" relationship in which the back of the left hand and forearm form a continuous line, (2) to establish left-side dominance, (3) to turn the shoulders on a sufficiently tilted plane to maintain the square hand-arm relationship with relative ease, and (4) to turn the shoulders as fully as possible.

During the waggle and the takeaway, the last three fingers of the left hand should curl under so as to establish the square relationship —the future impact position—of the left hand and lower forearm. This almost imperceptible move is made without any turning of the arm itself, and it establishes immediate control of the club with the left hand.

The clubhead should move straight back from the ball with the left arm fully extended. The clubhead will move inside the target line only as the shoulders begin to turn.

The right hand-arm-upper body should remain submissive as the left hand-arm-upper body "work under" the clubhead, moving it away and upward. There should be no independent lifting of the club by the hands and arms.

Pressure on the inside of the right foot should increase during the backswing, but should not move to the outside of this foot. The right knee should remain slightly flexed. The golfer should feel a gradual build-up of tension across his back and down his left arm and side and thigh.

At the top of the backswing the square hand-arm relationship should remain intact, and the left arm should remain extended. Resist temptation to relieve muscle tension by collapsing the back of the left wrist, loosening the left-hand grip, bending the left arm, increasing right-hand control, or rushing into the downswing.

Instead, seek to alleviate muscle strain by further developing the left hand, arm and side (see Chapter 6) and, possibly, by making your swing plane more upright through additional bending from the waist—but with your back straight—at address.

CHAPTER
FIVE

THE SQUARE-TO-SQUARE
DOWNSWING

Now we are ready to finish making our cake. We have gathered and measured the proper "ingredients" of grip and address position, and we have blended those ingredients during the backswing. All that remains is the downswing.

Those who teach the Square-to-Square Method feel that, compared to properly gripping, setting up and making the backswing, the downswing is relatively simple. It's as uncomplicated a procedure in making a golf shot as is the baking process in making a cake. All you must do is select the proper temperature setting and "turn on the oven."

The reason why making the downswing is much less involved than gripping, setting up and swinging back is simply because these steps required deliberate *action;* the downswing is largely an instinctive *reaction.*

For example, archery requires the *action* of sighting the target, the

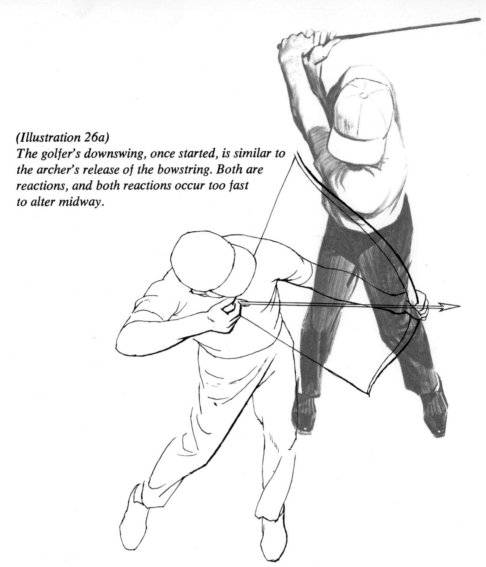

(Illustration 26a)
The golfer's downswing, once started, is similar to the archer's release of the bowstring. Both are reactions, and both reactions occur too fast to alter midway.

action of selecting the arrow, the *action* of fitting it to the bowstring, and the *actions* of pulling back the bowstring, aiming the arrow at the target, and letting go of the bowstring. Thereafter, everything is a *reaction* as the bowstring releases and projects the arrow forward.

So it is in the golf swing. Sighting the target is an *action*. So is gripping the club, putting the clubface squarely behind the ball, setting up in proper stance and posture, and making the backswing.

Then comes the start of the downswing, the "letting go of the bowstring." Everything that follows is a reaction. If you have aimed the club squarely, if you have gripped properly, if you have set up correctly, if you have made a good backswing, and if you have started down properly, then you will indeed make a fine shot—maybe even a "bull's-eye." No matter what happens during your downswing,

102

(Illustration 26b)
Upon completion of the initial move of the downswing,
the golfer will have prescribed, for better or for worse,
the path that his or her clubhead will follow through
the impact zone.

it cannot affect your shot. The success or failure of your shot is fore-ordained by everything that you did up to, and through, the start of your downswing. The cake has been made and the oven turned on, and your clubhead is moving too fast for you to alter its course.

GOALS OF THE DOWNSWING

Once started, the downswing pattern cannot be altered. The golfer cannot consciously re-direct his swing toward achieving any specific goals. There isn't enough time to re-route the swing. The club is moving so forcefully that no human has enough strength to change its course.

However, certain goals can be attained by *starting* the downswing correctly. These goals are: (1) to generate and retain as much club-head speed as possible through impact, (2) to pull the clubhead down and *along*—rather than *across*—the target line for as great a distance as possible in the impact area, and (3) to keep the clubface looking at the target as long as possible as it moves through this zone.

The golfer who can achieve these goals to the highest degree will, without doubt, make first class shots more consistently than will any other player.

HOW TO ACHIEVE THESE DOWNSWING GOALS

Those who teach the Square-to-Square swing feel that golfers are more likely to reach these goals if they regard the ideal downswing as being more of a pulling, rather than a *pushing,* of the clubhead. They feel that the best way to blend maximum clubhead speed, on-line clubhead path and on-target clubface alignment is to move the club with a continuous, sustained power that transmits from *in front* of the club during the downswing. This application of power from in front of the club is, of course, in opposition to thrusting or throw-ing or pushing the club from behind.

The golfer cannot pull the club on the downswing unless his or her left hand, arm and side remain in control. Once the right side becomes dominant, the downswing becomes a pushing or throwing action. When this takes place, several things occur that minimize chances of achieving the downswing goals.

First, when the right side takes over, the downswing begins incorrectly with an unwinding of the shoulders and a commensurate lowering of the hands and arms. To understand how this upsets the downswing, readers must recall that one of the goals of the backswing is to produce a maximum build-up of power by combining a maximum shoulder turn (on a tilted plane) with a minimum hip turn. This variation in degree of turning activates the big muscles

(Illustration 27)
To properly execute the Square-to-Square golf swing, right-handed golfers must learn to subordinate such "right-sided" tendencies as that of tossing a baseball. The downswing must be a pulling action of the lower-left side, rather than a pushing or throwing action of the upper-right side.

of the back and legs to a much greater extent than does a backswing in which both hips and shoulders turn about the same amount.

When the downswing begins with an unwinding of the shoulders, the degree of shoulder turn is, in effect, decreased *(illustration 28c)*. The difference between the amount of shoulder and hip turn is lessened. This premature unwinding of the shoulders dissipates energy in the form of clubhead speed. This energy could be better used if it came later in the downswing, as the clubhead moved into the impact zone.

The Square-to-Square Method, with its emphasis on left-side control, calls for the downswing to begin with a smooth lateral movement of the lower-left side of the body—below the thigh—to the left, while holding back the head and shoulders in the position they occupied at the completion of the backswing. This lateral movement of the lower-left quadrant puts the downswing into a pulling pattern with the lower left-side pulling the club, rather than a pushing pattern in which the upper-right side pushes it. This lateral movement must be a smooth reaction to the backswing wind-up, rather than a lurching or lashing action, so as to avoid putting too much pressure on the left hand.

When the downswing starts with a lowering of the left heel and a sideways movement of the left knee, the disparity between full shoulder turn and minimum hip turn remains intact until farther along in the downswing than was possible when the right side took over and forced the arms and shoulders to begin the downswing. If anything, starting the downswing with the lower-left side magnifies this disparity between minimum hip and full shoulder turn. Therefore, starting the downswing as a pulling action of the legs to the left, rather than as a throwing action with the arms and shoulders, retains, rather than dissipates, power *(illustrations 28a and 28b)*. Left-side control helps preserve clubhead speed until during impact when it's really needed.

PITFALL. *Care must be taken that the lateral shift to the*

STARTING DOWN

TOP-OF-SWING POSITION

(Illustration 28a)
Just before the start down, ideal top-of-swing position finds shoulders turned fully but hips turned minimally. This ideal, minimum hip turn is due largely to golfer's retaining a slight bend in his right knee throughout backswing—thus disallowing any swiveling of the hips—and his maintaining much of his weight on the inward portion of his right foot. The disparity between the degree of hip and shoulder turn has created maximum tension—power build-up—in the big muscles of the player's back and legs.

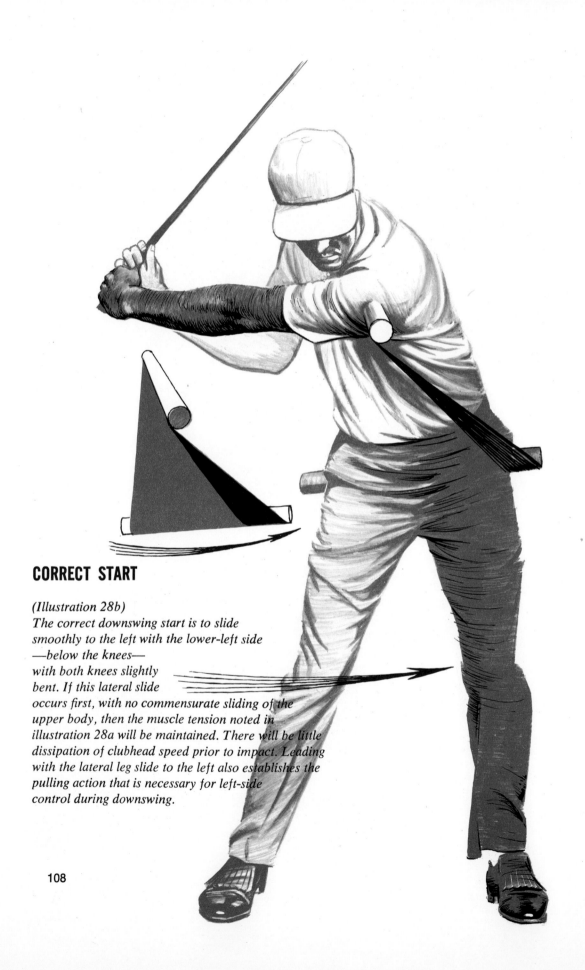

CORRECT START

(Illustration 28b)
The correct downswing start is to slide
smoothly to the left with the lower-left side
—below the knees—
with both knees slightly
bent. If this lateral slide
occurs first, with no commensurate sliding of the
upper body, then the muscle tension noted in
illustration 28a will be maintained. There will be little
dissipation of clubhead speed prior to impact. Leading
with the lateral leg slide to the left also establishes the
pulling action that is necessary for left-side
control during downswing.

108

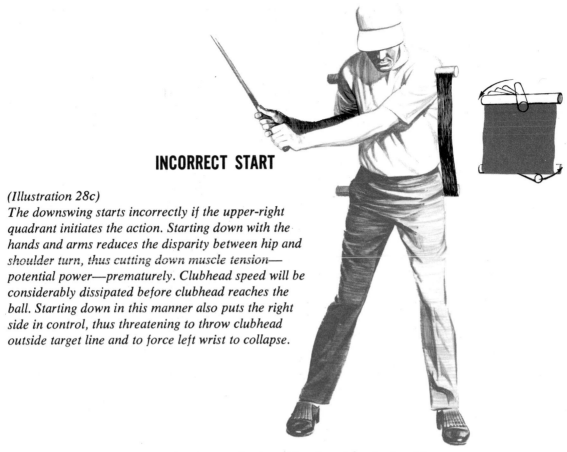

INCORRECT START

(Illustration 28c)
The downswing starts incorrectly if the upper-right quadrant initiates the action. Starting down with the hands and arms reduces the disparity between hip and shoulder turn, thus cutting down muscle tension—potential power—prematurely. Clubhead speed will be considerably dissipated before clubhead reaches the ball. Starting down in this manner also puts the right side in control, thus threatening to throw clubhead outside target line and to force left wrist to collapse.

left involve only the lower body. The head and shoulders must not be allowed to also shift laterally. The shoulders should be allowed to unwind, as will automatically occur, but they should not slide to the left.

PITFALL. *The lateral shift must be made with the left knee still flexed and leading the left hip. Should the hip rather than the knee lead, the leg will stiffen and cause the hips to spin instead of shift laterally. Such spinning of the hips tends to throw the clubhead outside the target line as the right shoulder swings out "over the ball."*

Another way that starting back with the lower-left quadrant increases clubhead speed at impact is by bringing the big muscles of the legs into the blow. The golfer who starts his or her downswing with the upper-body emphasizes the smaller, weaker arm muscles more so than does the golfer who first activates his or her legs and then, later, calls upon the upper body.

Moreover, pulling the right shoulder downward with a strong lower-left-side lead also momentarily "freezes" the right arm and wrist so that they cannot start to unhinge prematurely. This retains, rather than dissipates, clubhead speed for release later in the swing.

While teachers of Square-to-Square insist that the lower-left quadrant must start the downswing, they quickly add that the shoulders should, and will, unwind almost commensurately. They will unwind automatically as the lower-left quadrant pulls the right shoulder and arm downward. Thus, starting the downswing with a lateral pulling of the lower-left quadrant helps golfers best achieve the first downswing goal of increasing and preserving clubhead speed.

This same movement also helps golfers achieve the second downswing goal of pulling the clubhead *along*—rather than *across*—the target line for as long a duration as possible in the hitting area. As noted, to make a perfect golf shot, the clubhead must be moving along the target line when it impacts the ball. It is impossible to hit a straight shot that flies along the intended line if the clubhead is not moving in that direction during impact.

Again, instructors of the Square-to-Square swing feel that the best way to extend the distance that the clubhead moves along the target line is to pull, rather than push, the club during the downswing. And the best way to pull the club down to and through the ball is to start the downswing with a lateral movement of the lower-left quadrant to the left while keeping the head and shoulders in position.

To understand just why "left-side lead" improves chances of keeping the clubhead on line during impact, we must recall briefly the earlier discussion of swing plane. In that discussion it was established that the more vertical, or tilted, the swing plane—the more it matches the turning of a Ferris wheel—the greater will be the distance that the clubhead moves along the target line as it approaches and passes impact. The more horizontal the swing plane—the more it is like the turning of a merry-go-round—the shorter will be the distance that the clubhead moves along the target line in the impact zone.

Therefore, to achieve the downswing goal of keeping the club-head on line for maximum duration in the hitting area, the shoulders must unwind on a relatively tilted plane, just as they wound up on a relatively tilted plane during the backswing.

Those who teach Square-to-Square have found that the shoulders tend to unwind on too flat a plane if the downswing begins with the hands and arms and upper body. When this occurs the right hand, arm and shoulder *push* downward and outward at the start. The right shoulder starts to move out "over the ball," rather than down and under the chin. This flattened swing plane minimizes chances that the clubhead will move along the target line during impact.

Starting down with the upper-right side not only causes the shoulders to turn on a relatively level plane, but it also throws the clubhead outside the target line. Once the clubhead moves outside the line, it is impossible to return it along the line during impact. The only path it can possibly take is from outside to inside the line (*illustration 29b*). The normal result of this outside-in path is a pull-slice in which the ball starts left, because of the clubhead's path in that direction, and then bends right because of the clockwise spin that such a clubhead path imparts to the ball. Less frequently the outside-in clubhead path will cause a "pull" shot to the left, or a pull-hook. These off-line shots will occur if the clubhead is looking to the left of target, while moving from outside to inside the target line during impact.

Starting the downswing with the upper-right quadrant—right hand, arm and shoulder—also forces the right elbow and wrist to straighten prematurely. This "hitting from the top" uses up stored energy prematurely in the downswing and thus dissipates clubhead speed prior to impact.

On the other hand, those who teach Square-to-Square stress that starting the downswing with lateral movement of the lower-left quadrant *pulls* the right shoulder *downward*. This increases the duration that the clubhead moves along the target line because the properly

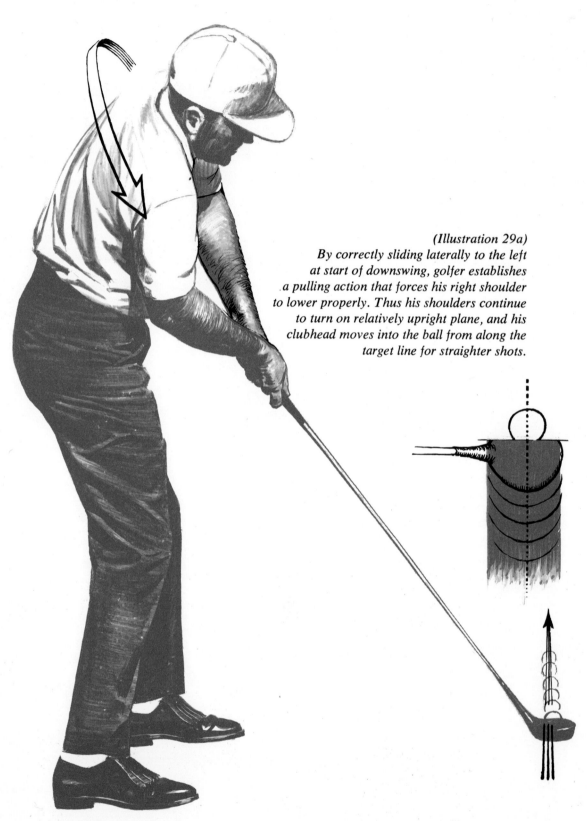

(Illustration 29a)
By correctly sliding laterally to the left
at start of downswing, golfer establishes
a pulling action that forces his right shoulder
to lower properly. Thus his shoulders continue
to turn on relatively upright plane, and his
clubhead moves into the ball from along the
target line for straighter shots.

112

tilted shoulder turn keeps the clubhead inside the target line. The clubhead moves into the ball from inside-to-along, rather than from outside-to-inside the target line *(illustrations 29a and 29b)*.

Again, those who teach the Square-to-Square Method stress that the golfer's ability to lead and pull with his lower-left side, depends largely on his ability to relax and restrain his right hand, arm and side. At the top of the backswing, especially, the temptation will be to let the right hand and arm and side ease the stress being applied to the left hand and arm and side. This temptation must be resisted if the downswing is to begin with a proper left-side pull, rather than a right-side push.

This strong left-side control also must be retained if you are to achieve the third of the three downswing goals, that being to keep the

(Illustration 29b)
When upper-right quadrant—hands and arms —start downswing, the right side takes over and forces the shoulders to turn on a too-level plane. This relatively level shoulder turn forces clubhead outside the target line so that it cannot return to ball along the target line; it must move across the line from outside to inside during impact.

113

clubface looking at the target as long as possible in the hitting area. Obviously, the longer the clubface looks down the target line, the better will be chances that it will be looking in that direction during the split second when the ball is on its surface.

Readers will recall that the Square-to-Square Method calls for the golfer to move the back of his or her left hand, wrist and lower forearm into the straight-line "square" position at the very start of the backswing by curling under the last three fingers of the left hand while moving the clubhead straight back from the ball.

Putting the hands and clubface into impact position during the takeaway, when the swing is slow-moving, is intended to eliminate the need to manipulate them into impact position either at the start of, or during, the faster-moving downswing when such manipulation requires split-second timing.

The square relationship of left hand and forearm, once established during the takeaway, must be retained during the downswing and through impact. It *will* be maintained so long as the right hand is not allowed to take over. If this should occur, the left wrist will weaken and collapse before or during impact *(illustration 30b)*. The stronger right hand will try to throw the clubhead into the ball and this will, inevitably, not only waste clubhead speed and move the clubhead off the line, but also open or close the clubface so that it no longer faces down the target line during impact.

In short, if the clubface is to be square during impact, the back of the left hand and forearm must continue to form a straight line as they swing down to, and through, the ball *(illustration 30a)*.

At the start of the downswing, as the lower-left quadrant shifts laterally to the left, the left hand must continue to dominate the hands' hold on the club. The left wrist should remain firm, welding the left hand and forearm in their straight-line impact relationship, as the lower body pulls the club down to the ball. Those who teach Square-to-Square note that the left wrist should never feel "springy" at the top of the swing or during impact.

Golfers should consciously seek to maintain the impact position

(Illustration 30b)
If the right side takes over on the downswing, the right hand will force the straight-line, square impact position of the left wrist to collapse before or during impact. This will force the clubface off line and reduce chances for straight shots. Weakening of the left wrist also dissipates clubhead speed and produces weak blows.

(Illustration 30a)
If the downswing is a pulling action with the left side leading and controlling, the straight-line, square impact position of the back of the left hand, wrist and lower forearm will be maintained until after the ball has been struck. Maintaining this square position through impact produces maximum opportunity for shots to fly straight and far.

115

of left hand and forearm until *past* impact. The back of the left hand and forearm should remain aligned and facing the target until *after* the ball has been struck. This is difficult for newcomers to the Square-to-Square swing to do because they lack sufficient strength in their left hand and arm to avoid any collapsing—bending inward—at the back of the wrist. Until their left-side control becomes stronger, many golfers' left wrist will collapse when the clubhead encounters the resistance of the ball. Overcoming this weakening of the left wrist will greatly increase chances that the clubface will remain on target through impact. Golfers who have developed excellent left-side control will be able to keep the line along the back of the left hand, wrist and lower forearm continuous until well into the follow-through. Photos of leading players, taken past impact, reveal this truth. They evidence no collapsing of the left wrist, which would indicate a takeover by the right side.

DOWNSWING CHECKPOINTS

Thus, those who teach the Square-to-Square Method regard the downswing as a pulling action with the lower-left quadrant shifting sideways to the left at the start. The shoulders begin to unwind on a tilted plane almost simultaneously as the left-side lead forces the right shoulder to start moving downward. The hands and club come last in this pulling action with the left hand and arm continuing to dominate the right side in controlling the club, thus preserving throughout the downswing the earlier-established, straight-line impact position of left hand and forearm.

Square-to-Square instructors would stress here the importance of leg action in the downswing. To retain left-side lead and left-side control, the legs, they stress, must both initiate the downswing by laterally shifting to the left and also continue the pulling action through impact.

As the knees drive forward to the left, they should continue to remain flexed. Top players almost appear to be "sitting down" during their downswing. At impact the outside edge of the left knee

normally will have moved so far to the left that it will be out beyond
—ahead of—the left hip. The golfer should never feel a stiffening
of the left leg during impact. This would indicate that the arms and
shoulders, rather than the lower-left quadrant, started the downswing.

When the legs properly lead the downswing by driving to the left,
and when the left hand remains firmly in control of the club, the
golfer should feel that the back of his left hand is looking downward,
towards the ball, as opposed to out or up, as he approaches impact.
He also may feel that his clubhead will never "catch up" in time for
it to be looking at the target during impact. He will feel that his left
hand and side are pulling the clubhead through the ball and that his
hands are too far ahead of his clubhead. There may be some tendency to hold back the hands so that the clubhead can catch up. This
tendency should be resisted.

This feeling that the clubhead is lagging is understandable and
normal—and even desirable. It indicates that the left side is still in
control, that potential clubhead speed is being retained rather than
dissipated. Scientists have measured clubhead speed by studying high-
speed stroboscopic photos of golfers swinging. They have established
beyond question that even expert golfers produce their maximum
clubhead speed at a point *before* impact. This maximum release of
energy in the form of clubhead speed occurs before the clubhead
reaches the ball because no human yet tested has been able to hold
back the full release of maximum centrifugal force until impact. However, those golfers who hit the ball exceptionally long distances do
produce their maximum clubhead speed *very close* to impact. The
clubhead slowdown before it reaches the ball is very slight. Lesser-
skilled golfers, those who allow the right side to take over, release
their maximum power earlier in their downswings. They lose more
clubhead speed before impact. The farther the hands lead the clubhead, the longer maximum clubhead speed will be retained.

Stop-action photos of good players show this leading of the clubhead with the hands at impact. The back of the left wrist is slightly
ahead of the back of the hand in many instances. In effect, the back

of the left hand is still looking slightly downward, as well as towards the target. Though such convexity of the back of the left wrist indicates a slight departure from the square—straight-line—hand-forearm relationship, those who teach the Square-to-Square swing encourage such an impact position. They regard it as further indication that the left hand and arm and side have remained dominant and are pulling the club through the ball.

These instructors further advise that golfers not concern themselves if their hands are slightly ahead of the clubhead at impact, so long as the back of the left hand and forearm are both looking at the target. Shots struck with the hands leading the clubhead will fly a bit lower than normal, because of the decreased loft of the clubface, but they will fly straight and in the direction that the clubhead is moving during impact.

One of the assets of the Square-to-Square swing is that the golfer can drive forward with his legs as forcefully as possible so long as his left wrist remains firm through impact. Golfers can swing at full force with no need to "block out"—consciously slow down the hands or the hips—in order to avoid hooking. So long as the left wrist remains firm and straight, and so long as the club moves along the target line during impact, there is no way a golfer who successfully employs the Square-to-Square Method can hook. Hooking will occur only if the clubhead varies from its proper path, or if the left wrist collapses and bends inward, thus closing the clubface, before or during impact.

Except for trying to retain the firm left-wrist position, the golfer need not be concerned with movements or positions during his follow-through.

The follow-through is pre-ordained by earlier stages of the swing, including the setting up to the ball. If the golfer has turned his shoulders on a sufficiently upright plane, and if he has maintained sufficient left-side control, he will find that his hands automatically will move into a nice high finish position. He will feel that he is looking at the shot from "under," rather than "over," the ball.

SUMMARY

The goals of the downswing are to move the clubhead through the ball (1) at maximum speed, (2) along the target line and (3) with the clubface looking at the target. These goals are best achieved if the left side controls the downswing by pulling the club, as opposed to the right side pushing or throwing it.

The downswing begins with a lateral shifting of the lower-left side, below the thigh, to the left. This movement forces the right shoulder to lower on a sufficiently tilted plane to keep the club inside the target line and to preserve left hand-arm control throughout the downswing. The legs continue to drive forward to the left, pulling the shoulders, arms and club downward, while the head stays back in its original position. Throughout the downswing the left hand and arm should remain in firm control with no feeling of springiness. At impact the back of the left hand and forearm should be facing the target and moving parallel to the target line. The back of the hand may be turned slightly downward, if the hands lead the clubhead, but it should never look upward or face out to the right of target. The left wrist should remain firm through impact and into the follow-through.

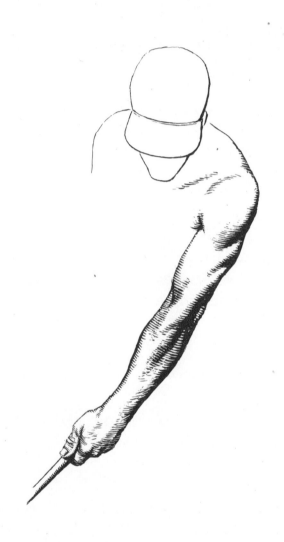

CHAPTER
SIX

BUILDING SQUARE-TO-SQUARE MUSCLES

Those who teach the Square-to-Square Method stress that swinging a golf club *properly* is indeed a highly physical act. Even accomplished professionals, who are accustomed to practicing and playing almost daily, admit to feeling weary after hitting 100 or so full shots during an intensive session on the practice range. And no wonder. Scientists have calculated that a top golfer accelerates his clubhead from 0 to about 100 miles per hour during the fraction of a second that elapses during the downswing—or about 100 times faster acceleration than the fastest sports car can muster.

Proper technique, as outlined in the preceding pages, allows a golfer to derive maximum benefit from whatever muscle power he or she can command. Proper technique brings the strongest muscles into play in a manner that transfers body energy into clubhead speed with a minimum of wasted effort. Square-to-Square instructors note, however, that proper technique will take a golfer only so far. To achieve maximum proficiency, somewhere along the way the player must supplement proper technique with the development of strength through simple exercise.

Specifically the Square-to-Square Method requires strengthening those muscles that are needed to control the club with the left side and to pull, rather than push, the club during the downswing.

Unfortunately, most golfers are right-side oriented (left handers usually are left-side oriented). Through day-to-day living over the years, right-handed people unconsciously build up the right hand, arm and side through a multiplicity of conscious and unconscious actions—opening doors, unscrewing bottle caps, throwing baseballs, swinging tennis racquets, sweeping floors, polishing windows, etc. It is only natural that the right side also dominate the right-hander's golf swing.

Because muscles of the stronger right side naturally dominate

most golf swings, those who teach the Square-to-Square Method feel that the *proper* golf swing is not a "natural" act. In the Square-to-Square swing, as noted in earlier chapters, the weaker left side must dominate the right, and this is *unnatural*. The weaker left side must dominate from the start of the backswing so that the clubhead is pushed out and back along the target line, rather than lifted abruptly with the right hand. The weaker left side must dominate the upper backswing because right-side tension in the arm and shoulder prohibits making a full shoulder turn on a properly tilted plane. The lower-left side must start the downswing, thus preventing the upper-right side from throwing the club to the outside and prematurely releasing clubhead speed. The weaker left side must pull the clubhead through the ball in order to maintain square clubface alignment through impact.

Thus, the Square-to-Square Method requires a "re-training" of

(Illustration 31)
*Swinging with only the left hand is the best way to develop
proper muscles to fully implement Square-to-Square Method. Be sure to
address ball with proper posture and with pressure in last three fingers of
left hand dominant. Take the clubhead back along the target line while
curling under to form straight-line square position at back of left hand,*

the golfer's muscle structure. The muscles of the weaker left hand
and arm and side must be taught to dominate their stronger counter-
parts on the right side. The Method also requires a strengthening of
leg muscles so that they properly initiate a forceful pull during the
downswing.

During the early stages of learning the Method, the average
golfer surely will find it difficult to relinquish right-side control and
to teach his or her left side to dominate. Most golfers will experience
soreness because they are using "new" muscles. This soreness is to be
expected—even cherished—for it indicates that the left side is learning to take over.

*wrist and lower forearm. Make a full shoulder turn with left arm fully
extended, but minimize hip turn by keeping right knee bent and weight
inward on right foot. Start downswing with lateral sliding of the lower-
left quadrant to the left with both knees still bent. Pull club through
impact zone with left wrist remaining firm until well into follow-through.*

SQUARE-TO-SQUARE EXERCISES

The best way to strengthen the muscles of the left side, and to
train them to dominate the swing, is simply to practice swinging
while holding onto the club with only the left hand. Here is the
procedure:

1. Assume the proper left-hand grip and correct set-up position.
Emphasize pressure in the last three fingers. Make sure that you bend
sufficiently from the waist, with your back straight, so that you must
"look back" to see your hands. Your lower back should feel "hollow."

2. Make your backswing with your arm fully extended and the
clubhead moving straight back from the ball. Don't forget to "curl

under" to set your hand-forearm relationship into the straight-line "square impact" position. Turn your shoulders on a tilted plane so that your left hand is "high" and left arm still extended at the top of your swing. Keep your right knee flexed.

3. Start your downswing with your knees—still flexed—shifting laterally to the left, thus pulling your right shoulder downward on a sufficiently vertical plane.

4. Pull the clubhead through the "ball" with the back of your hand and forearm facing the target. Retain strength in your last three fingers until you finish your swing.

Practice swinging in this manner during once-daily sessions. During each session, swing until your muscles feel tired. At first this tiredness may occur after just a few swings. Later you will be able to swing longer, perhaps up to five minutes, pausing only a few seconds between swings.

Some golfers, especially women, will find it difficult at first to swing properly with a driver. Their arm will bend at the top of the swing, or their wrist will collapse inward so that wrinkles appear below the back of the hand. If this should occur, practice swinging a shorter-shafted club for a time. Gradually work up to longer-shafted clubs without increasing the number of swings from day to day. Once you can swing the driver, then increase the number of swings as your strength increases.

Those who teach the Square-to-Square Method agree that this single drill will improve any golfer, even if he or she is unwilling to devote the time and effort necessary to carry out the Method itself to the nth degree. It will benefit any player, whether he or she be the player who is seeking to lower average scores from 120 to 115 or from 75 to 70. Teachers of the Method stress, however, that there is a more or less direct correlation between improved scoring and the degree that the left-side muscles are trained to dominate the swing.

While swinging the club with only the left hand is the best way to develop and train those muscles needed under the Square-to-

Square Method, golfers who seek maximum distance and club control should further develop their legs and strengthen their left-hand grip through additional exercise. Skipping rope is the method most-advocated for adding both strength and speed of movement to the legs. Squeezing a golf club or a similarly shaped object, such as a rubber dog bone, with the left hand—especially the last three fingers —will do wonders for improving club control.

Finally, those who teach the Method advise that you study top players, either in person, on television or in golf magazines. Note especially how well these players establish and maintain the "square impact" relationship with the back of their left hand and forearm until well through impact. Check how well these players extend their left arm during their backswing and turn their shoulders fully, usually on a relatively upright plane. Finally, study how these fine players pull the club downward to the ball with their lower-left quadrant leading the way.

Disciples of the Square-to-Square Method point out that the swings of today's outstanding players do indeed reflect the techniques that they advocate. Thus their swings serve as models for the modern golfer. These teachers firmly believe that with diligent application of the techniques described in this book, you too can develop a model swing for others to follow.